THE BULFINCH
GUIDE TO
CARPETS

Enza Milanesi

THE BULFINCH GUIDE TO
CARPETS

HOW TO IDENTIFY, CLASSIFY, AND EVALUATE ANTIQUE ORIENTAL CARPETS AND RUGS

A Bulfinch Press Book
Little, Brown and Company
Boston • New York • Toronto • London

First North American Edition
Second printing, 1997

ISBN 0-8212-2057-8
Library of Congress Catalog Card Number: 9372046

Translation by Jay Hyams

Bulfinch Press is an imprint and trademark of Little, Brown and Company (Inc.)
Published simultaneously in Canada by Little, Brown & Company (Canada) Limited

Printed in Spain by Artes Gráficas Toledo, S.A.
D.L.TO: 966-1997

CONTENTS

INTRODUCTION

Antique Oriental carpets are hard to resist. Immediately drawn to the beauty of their designs and colours, we find ourselves fascinated by an exotic creation: the foreign decorations, the unusual compositions, the somber or gaudy shades, the ancient and unfamiliar technique all lend such carpets a sense of the unknown and the mysterious. This guide attempts to unveil some of the mystery without diminishing any of the fascination of these carpets. Understanding stylistic characteristics (of both decoration and technique) and using them to identify a given specimen—to determine its area of production—is a process that can only increase our enjoyment of these products. The Guide to Carpets is designed to provide precisely those necessary basics, the simple and straightforward tools that are required to recognize the stylistic characteristics of carpets.

The first section explains the general concepts of carpet styles and their identification; it examines the practical and artistic functions of carpets as well as their theoretical and technical development. It then explores in depth decoration, the arrangement of designs, and the most frequent ornamental motifs and how they have been interpreted in geometric or curvilinear styles in relation to the four cultural spheres of production (nomadic, village, city, and great atelier).

The second section examines in detail the important geographical areas of production: Anatolia, Persia, Caucasus, central Asia (western and eastern Turkestan), India, China, and the few places in Europe of historical importance to carpets. Each of these areas is analyzed historically, from the earliest antique types (dating from the beginning of carpet making to 1860-1870) to semi-antique or old carpets (those from 1860-1870 to 1920-1930), as they were made in the principal centers of production. Special attention is devoted to these production centers because the typical characteristics of each one provide the basic information used to recognize individual carpets, and such recognition involves identifying the carpet with the name of a specific center: a Kerman, for example, possesses stylistic characteristics found only in Kerman and not in any other city. All of this information is illustrated with photographs, maps, and drawings, and the major geographical production areas (Anatolia, Persia, Caucasus, and central Asia) are furnished with special comparison tables that make the specific qualities of every center and every principal type clear and easy to remember.

The knowledge necessary to recognize a type of carpet and identify it with a precise name is not easy to come by, but just being able to determine the geographical origins of a carpet by "reading" it and correctly interpreting its stylistic characteristics is itself a great achievement and a source of much satisfaction.

HOW TO APPROACH THE WORLD OF CARPETS

♦ When we think of carpets, we think of the Orient. This seems like a cliché, but it is natural that we rarely think of connecting the word *carpet* with the West. European carpets such as Aubusson or Savonnerie, for example, are of less importance and are less well-known than those of the East. This situation is understandable for it was in the Orient that the carpet was born and developed, where it represented at once both a fundamental object of daily life and one of the highest artistic expressions. Most of this book is dedicated to Oriental carpets, and in particular to those classified as antique and old, products that date to before around 1920, which is to say those carpets not yet contaminated by the new requirements born from trade with Europe and America.

In the West, we use these fascinating articles in our homes only as elements of furnishing, usually as floor decorations that are often hidden beneath other furniture; in much of the East, however, carpets have always represented the focus of the house as well as a sanctuary, the place where one bows down five times a day in prayer. Every carpet should be considered within this context, for doing so not only restores the carpet's

true cultural value but also permits us to "read" its artistic importance from the correct point of view.

The concept of style in carpets

How does one approach an expression of art and culture that is so different from

one's own? In the absence of Western standards and aesthetic categories, how can one formulate judgments? In examining a painting, for example, we are aided by the traditional Western concepts of space, perspective, and proportion, etc., and we usually know something about the artist or at least about the particular artistic period of the work. A carpet does not fit such criteria and, except for a few cases, is absolutely anonymous, precisely because from the beginning carpets were conceived as living things made to be used and not simply to be displayed and admired.

The first thing one must recognize when examining a carpet is that carpet decoration is based on two concrete elements: design and colour. The design may be more or less elementary or complex, the colour more or less uniform or varied, but it is the relationship between design and colour that determines the style— the character or spirit—of the carpet.

The compositional designs and decorative motifs of ' Oriental carpets have remained the same over the centuries, but the ways of interpreting and connecting them as well as the colours

employed have given life to many diverse styles according to period and geographical area. At least four basic characteristics can be established. These are tied to the four major types of production center: the context of the nomadic tribe, the small village workshop, the specialized city workshop, and finally the great court atelier. The character of carpets has changed from time to time according to whether the carpets were made for commercial purposes and to the decorative traditions of where they were made, but also according to the type of loom used (horizontal or vertical), the nature of the material employed, and the kind of knot used. In general, carpets made by nomadic tribes are naïve, based on simple geometric forms and a few contrasting colours; those from village workshops are somewhat more elaborate, based on

abstract or stylized geometric designs, and their colours are more varied; those from city workshops are complex or refined and employ many different geometric, stylized, or floral designs, with the use of many colours always matched harmoniously; and those from court ateliers are extremely sumptuous and sophisticated, with the use of highly complex, geometric, and above all curvilinear designs and with greatly varied colours harmoniously matched.

The style of a carpet is determined by the concrete relationship between design and colour, but that relationship is decisively affected by the environment in which the carpet was produced, for the cultural traditions and techniques employed in an environment establish, according to the period, the designs and colours. To approach a carpet correctly involves

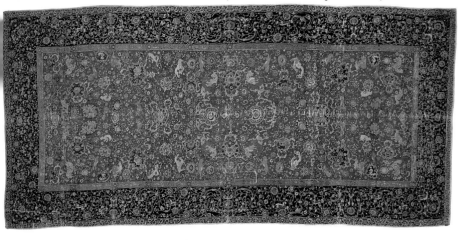

9

Tekke carpet; western Turkestan, end 19th century. The style of decoration of this carpet is known in the West as the Bukhara design, but in reality it is characteristic of carpets made by a number of nomadic Turkoman tribes, mainly the Tekke.

taking every component into consideration: function, style, decoration, the context in which the carpet was made, and also its origins, history, and technique.

Style and the identification of carpets

Conventionally speaking, identifying a carpet means attributing to it a provenance, or zone of production. The various combinations of designs and colours have permitted the determination of decorative types that are useful for the purposes of classification, but this does not mean there are fixed rules or that problems do not arise, for styles do not always correspond to single, precise provenances. Confusion is also generated by misleading conventional uses, as is the case with the so-called Bukhara design, which was created not in the city of Bukhara but by nomadic Turkoman tribes spread across central Asia; Bukhara was only the collection and marketing center of these carpets. The identification of a carpet is thus not easy. The designs and colours must be compared with those typical of the presumed place of manufacture, and both the invariable elements and the character of the variants must be taken into consideration in order to define the predominant elements of a given carpet. Identifying the decorative type does not provide the most correct method of classification. One must never forget to examine the characteristics of the material used and any particularities of technique: the number of weft strands between one row of knots and the next, any colouring of the weft strands, the style of the fringe, the type of knot, and so on. Such elements can be fundamental in attributing a carpet to one geographical area instead of another. In general, given the difficulties involved in identifying carpets, it is better to reserve judgment than plunge ahead on questionable ground.

THE CARPET BETWEEN REALITY AND THEORY

♦ By *carpet* we usually mean the knotted carpet, a particular decorative textile made by hand on a horizontal or vertical loom using the technique of knotting to obtain not an ordinary flat fabric but an artificial pile that hides the supporting foundation, or framework. This foundation is composed of the grid formed by the crossing of horizontal strands (warp) with vertical strands (weft). The technique of knotting involves the creation of horizontal rows of knots across the width of the carpet. Each knot is created by looping a length of yarn through warp strands (usually two adjacent strands). The two ends of the inserted yarn are left protruding and when cut create a characteristic "tuft"; the many tufts formed by the rows of knots create the surface, or pile, of the carpet. Decoration is created by using strands of different colours for the knots, following a procedure in which each knot is very much like a coloured tile in a mosaic. Carpets can be knotted in several ways, but the primary materials are always the same and include wool, cotton, or— for the most precious examples—silk. Such natural fibers are highly subject to deterioration; wool, in particular, with the passing of time crystallizes

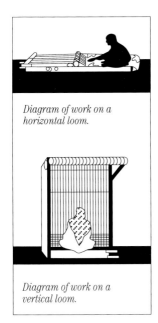

Diagram of work on a horizontal loom.

Diagram of work on a vertical loom.

and turns to powder. The highly perishable nature of the primary materials of carpets does not favour their preservation and explains the scarcity of solid evidence from the past. It also has had fundamental consequences on the criteria used in the chronological classification of carpets as well on the definitions of carpets used in the antique trade.

Mysterious origins

Because of the absence of documentary evidence, the basic questions of where and why the knotted carpet was born have never been fully resolved. Even so, two theories concerning the origins of the knotted carpet have been put forward. According to the first of

these, the knotted carpet came into being during an early period and was created by rough, nomadic populations seeking a way to protect themselves from direct contact with the ground without sacrificing the skins of their precious animals. The first carpets came into being on rudimentary horizontal looms, easily dismantled and transported, and had the utilitarian aim of providing an artificial pile that could replace the natural skins of sheep and goats with which these peoples warmed themselves and that could be used to avoid direct contact with the ground. The original intentions were thus exclusively practical and not artistic; only after the passage of time did aesthetic interest come into being, and the desire to use these special fabrics to decorate tent interiors led to an increase in the variety of the colours and designs used, which then evolved into established decorative motifs. According to this theory, these nomadic populations introduced the carpet to the populations of villages and cities, who appropriated it.

The supporters of the second theory agree that the knotted carpet came into being at an early age, but believe it was created during a more evolved period and among settled peoples already familiar

THE CARPET BETWEEN REALITY AND THEORY

with the vertical loom. According to this theory, the carpet was created in response to a precise aesthetic need, the desire to decorate the interiors of permanent dwellings. From its origins, the carpet thus served artistic goals connected to celebratory and ceremonial aims. Only later did nomadic peoples appropriate this new product, rendering rougher and more primitive versions because they used horizontal looms, a result of their adapting the more evolved vertical loom to their different way of life.

An important archaeological discovery of 1947 can be taken as support for the second theory. Excavations of the tomb of a Shiite chief in the Pazyryk valley of the Altai mountains in Siberia uncovered a beautiful wool carpet, knotted and thickly decorated, that had been encased in a block of ice and was thus perfectly preserved. Two repeating design patterns stand out from its decoration: the first is a series of horsemen; the second a row of elk. Datable to the 5th century B.C., the Pazyryk carpet is the oldest known ancient carpet, and its refined workmanship seems to confirm the hypothesis that carpets served artistic uses from their very beginnings. All theories aside, nothing

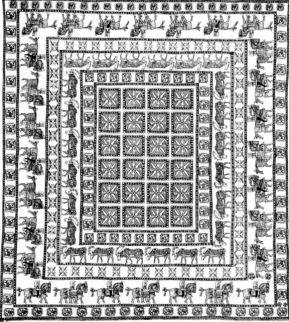

rules out the possibility that knotted carpets came into being at some early time and served both to protect people from the cold ground and to give aesthetic pleasure by decorating the interior of dwellings, rendering them more inviting.

The place of origin

The place where carpets originated remains shrouded in mystery because of the widespread use of the knotted carpet throughout the Middle East. The strongest argument holds that Turkestan in central Asia was the cradle of carpet-making, for carpet fragments have been found there datable to the 2nd-3rd century B.C., the oldest after the Pazyryk carpet. Peoples migrating from Turkestan then spread this form of textile to the west to Persia, the Causasus, and Anatolia, to the east to China, and later to the south to India.

The carpet as a "living" object

The carpet has assumed a profound significance in the Islamic world and has undergone remarkable development. In his *Travels*, written near the end of the 13th century, Marco Polo says of the people of Turkey that "They weave the choicest and most beautiful carpets in the world." As both a means of artistic expression and a sacred area, the carpet has evolved within Islamic culture, becoming increasingly important to daily life. Called by the Persians *khali*, meaning

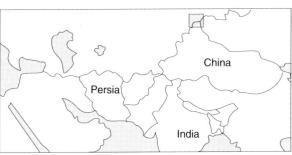

"what is stepped on," it has been given its own complex meaning as a "living" object made to be used and therefore ultimately destined to be consumed or ruined. The rather short life of the carpet with respect to other artistic genres not only explains the true rarity of older examples but also justifies the application to carpets of a special type of chronological classification, one wider and less rigid than those normally applied to other art objects.

Chronological classification

All carpets made before circa 1920 are included within the category of antiques, but the classification is more precise: *antique* carpets are generally defined as traditional examples produced before the introduction of chemical dyes, which occurred in the period 1860-1870; *semi-antique* or *old* carpets are those made from 1860-1870 to the early 20th century, in

which the traditional characteristics, although prevalent, have been partially modified in response to new commercial needs. Next are *modern* carpets, those produced since 1920-1930, which show total conformity to market demands, especially demands from the West, to the clear detriment of quality and tradition.

This classification system is quite elementary, and the definition of an antique carpet spreads across a wide chronological band. It should be pointed out, however, that antique specimens and those made before 1800 in general are so rare that they can be found today only in museums or large collections, and the remains from the 16th and 17th centuries are for the most part only fragments. The carpets on the market today are primarily from the 19th and early 20th centuries, for these are the carpets most likely to have been preserved.

13

STRUCTURE AND MANUFACTURE

♦ The primary materials of carpets have been the same for centuries: wool, cotton, and silk, to which can be added silver and gold thread, although these have been used only for exceptional carpets, those made for shahs and emperors. The materials used, of course, have always depended on their availability in a given production area and on the requirements the final product was designed to meet. Because of its availability throughout the Orient, wool is the most widely used carpet-making fiber. Sheep wool is preferred, but goat hair has also been used and, in sporadic cases, camel hair, although it is less durable and is particularly resistant to dyes. In antique carpets and those made by nomads, wool is used for both the pile and the underlying foundation, while in old and modern production it is given only the privileged role of forming the pile.

Being a strong material that holds it shape, cotton is particularly well suited to support the tension applied to the inner structures of carpets and is therefore used for carpet foundations; it is sometimes used for the pile, but only to create white areas. Requiring cultivation by settled populations or at least organized commercial availability, cotton, unlike wool, is not part of the production of nomads but is normally used in city and village workshops.

Silk is the most costly and precious material because of its softness and shine and also because, being particularly thin, it can be used to make exceptionally fine knots, permitting the creation of highly refined products. Used exclusively by city workshops that specialized in making carpets on order, silk is used most of all in the pile, alone or combined with wool, to make a particular area of a design stand out. In the past it was also used for the foundations of rare, and decidedly luxurious, examples. Wool, cotton, and silk are spun into thread by twisting the fibers, which can be done clockwise or counter-clockwise; by convention, clockwise twisting is called Z twisting and counter-clockwise is called S. Analysis of twisting can help identify carpets.

The weft strands are usually of the same material as the warp, but they may be more loosely spun and may also be dyed; the presence of dyed weft strands and their particular colours are an important element in carpet identification.

Colours and dyes

The next step in the manufacture of a carpet is dyeing the threads, a delicate operation traditionally performed by men. Until 1860-1870 natural dyes were used exclusively; after that date new chemical dyes began to appear, and because of their ease of use and low prices these eventually replaced the natural dyes. Natural dyes, made by master dyers following secret formulas, were composed of substances found in nature, such as saffron crocus, pomegranate skins, or vine leaves for yellow; cochineal (the dried bodies of female cochineal insects), cherry juice, or madder for red; indigo for blue; and nutshells, tobacco, or tea for black and brown. Having obtained primary colours, complementary colours could be created by further baths in two or more colours.

Natural dyeing involved long and costly procedures, so when new chemical dyes became available from Europe between 1860-1870 they enjoyed an immediate success. This is why these years constitute an important reference point in the chronological classification of carpets.

The first chemical dyes were aniline dyes that resisted light poorly and damaged fibers. Their use was banned in Persia in 1890 by order of the shah. Early in the 20th century, these aniline dyes were

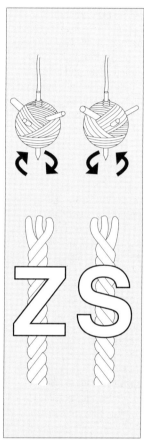

STRUCTURE AND MANUFACTURE

replaced by chrome dyes, which were completely reliable and available in a wide range of tones.

Particular mention must be made of abrashes, variations in the intensity or tone of a given colour in the ground of a carpet. These chromatic irregularities are caused by a difference in the absorption of dye by some of the fibers or by the use of a batch of yarn of the same tint but not from the same dye bath. Abrashes sometimes reveal themselves over time, and sometimes they are purposefully made by the weaver to confer a kind of guarantee of artisan authenticity to the carpet. The maker might also desire to liven up a single background colour, which might otherwise seem too uniform to Oriental taste, by making it more vibrant.

The loom

The loom is an indispensable tool in the creation of a carpet since it holds the numerous warp strands secure during work. Two kinds of loom are used, horizontal and vertical, and both follow the same principle: they hold the warp strands tight and secure between two parallel beams—always kept at an established distance—to permit the passage of the weft strands and thus the assembly of the foundation.

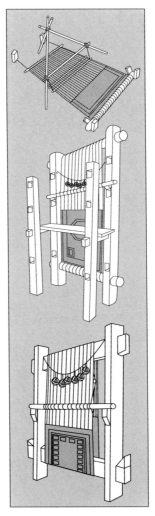

The horizontal loom, smaller than the vertical and more primitive, is placed flat on the ground, almost in contact with it. Horizontal looms are used by nomadic tribes because they can be easily assembled and dismantled, even when work has begun on a carpet, simply by rolling the part of the carpet

already completed. Made small to facilitate transportation, they permit the creation only of medium or small carpets, for the size of the carpet cannot exceed that of the loom itself.

More complicated than the horizontal, the vertical loom is used by settled peoples in villages and cities for, aside from requiring solid support structures, it is itself a construction with a fixed character. Three kinds are in general use. The first and most elementary has fixed beams and is used to make carpets whose length cannot exceed the height of the loom; since the work proceeds from the bottom upward the weaver must change position upward by readjusting a movable bench. The second type, known as the Tabriz loom, has a movable lower beam and has the warp strands arranged along a double loom so that the finished work can be slid to the rear. This permits the creation of carpets that are twice the length of the height of the loom and also permits the weaver to stay in one place throughout the process. The third type, known as a roller loom, has rotating beams that unwind long warp strands from the upper beam that are then wound onto the lower beam as the work progresses, permitting the creation of very wide carpets. Such roller looms were put to much use in the great court ateliers of the past.

Knots

The knotting that distinguishes this particular type of textile is traditionally entrusted to women and even young girls, although the work was performed exclusively by men in royal workshops. The work proceeds horizontally, advancing from one end of the loom to the other. Two basic kinds of knot have always been used in the Orient: the first is the symmetrical, or Ghiordes, knot, also known as the Turkish knot because it was used most widely in Turkey; the second is the asymmetrical, or Senneh, knot, also known as the Persian knot because it was used for the most part in Persia. Regardless of these names, there is no clear-cut geographical distribution of the two knot types; both are practiced everywhere, so much so that the Turkish knot is traditionally used in the Persian city of Senneh (today's Sanadaj). Even so, a certain stylistic distribution can be observed, since in general the symmetrical knot, being larger and square, is more adapted to the creation of geometrical designs, while the asymmetrical knot, smaller and irregular, is better adapted to

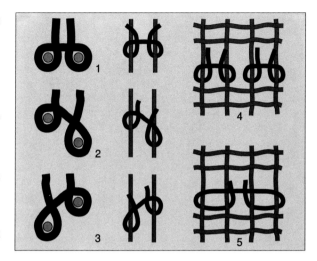

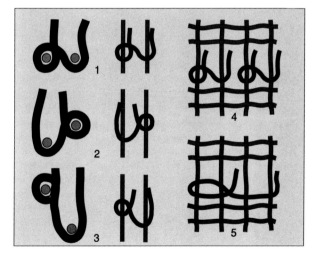

curvilinear motifs. Technically, both knots usually involve two strands of the warp at a time. In the symmetrical, or Ghiordes, knot, the yarn is wrapped around both warp strands, and then the two ends are looped around the warp strands and drawn back out to protrude between the strands. The pair of free ends forms a "tuft" of the pile. In the asymmetrical, or Senneh, knot, the yarn is wound around one warp strand and then looped under and drawn back around the other, leaving the two ends of the "tuft" separated by the one free strand. Since the pile yarn can be drawn either to the left or the right, knots are said to be "open" to the left or right according to which strand is wrapped. The difference between the symmetrical and asymmetrical systems can be observed by folding the pile of a carpet horizontally in the direction of the weft and examining a row of knots. In addition to these principal systems, a variant system has been used, known as the jufti knot, in which the pile yarn is wrapped around four warp strands rather than two. Also known as the "false" knot, this system was used during recent times to increase the speed of weaving although it produces inferior, less durable carpets. The jufti knot was derived from an ancient traditional practice of Khorasan used to achieve particular effects of emphasis. A fourth ancient type of knotting, almost unknown in the Orient but much used in Spain, is the single-warp knot, better known as the Spanish knot. In this system the pile yarn is wrapped around a single thread of the warp, alternating even and odd, leaving the two free ends of the knot at the sides of the warp.

The number of knots that have been tied per square inch of the pile of a carpet determines the fineness of the knotting. In general, the more the knots the finer the knotting, but a higher density of knots is not necessarily an indication of

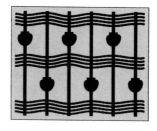

greater quality. Knot density can, however, serve as an indication of where a carpet was made.

Carpet making

The basic principal of carpet making involves alternating a horizontal row of knots with one or more rows (passed) of weft; continuous rows of knots and weft are worked across the entire width of the loom. Having stretched the warp strands on the loom, the weaver makes each row of knots, using a hooked knife to form each knot. Each row of

knots is usually followed by two passed rows of weft that serve to align the knots and reinforce the structure. The weaver then tightens the weft strands against the rows of knots by beating against them with special wooden or metal combs.

The colours of the knots are determined by the design being made.

Having knotted the entire carpet, the ends of the warp strands are cut from the loom to take the carpet off the loom. (The ends of the warp strands are tied or woven in various ways to form the fringe.) The next step in completing the carpet is clipping the pile, an important process performed by specialized workers who use flat shears to cut the pile to the desired height or to the height prescribed by tradition.

The carpet is then washed

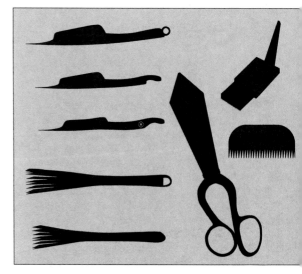

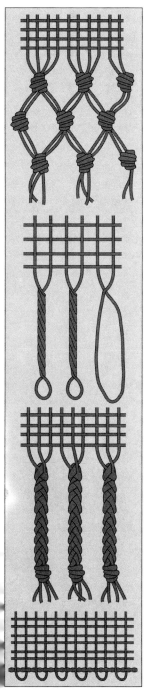

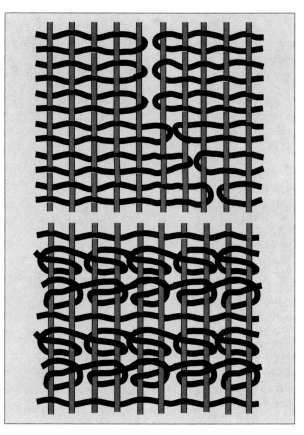

Kilims and soumaks

in running water to settle and soften the structure and then dried in the sun to set the colours and fade tints that are too bright.

In addition to knotted carpets, flatwoven rugs have been made in the Orient for many centuries. These rugs have neither knots nor pile; instead, the weft strands (serving a decorative role rather than the structural role of knotted carpets) are threaded through a number of warp strands and then looped back, much as in Western tapestry weaving. The surface of the carpet is therefore flat. Flatwoven rugs are known as kilims (Turkish) or gelims (Persian) and soumaks, according to the method used.

Flatweaving techniques have been practiced primarily by nomadic peoples, who have employed them in the creation of articles of daily use, such as sacks, cushions, saddle cloths, and blankets.

DECORATION
AND STYLE

◆ The vast majority of
Oriental carpets are
rectangular, and their
decoration is usually
arranged in accordance
with established rules of
composition, or layouts.
These layouts involve every
area of the surface, which
is divided into a central
area, or field, with corners
and surrounding borders.
The layouts can be
directional, nondirectional,
or centralized.

Directional layouts are
arranged according to a
single axis of symmetry and
are thus made to be looked
at from one particular
direction. Certain figural
carpets, such as garden or
animal designs, can be
structured in this way, but
the most eloquent
examples are prayer rugs.
Prayer rugs provide the
faithful Muslim with a
clean area away from the
ground, which is held to be
impure, on which to pray,
and their designs help the
Muslim orient his position
and thus his prayers
toward the holy city of
Mecca. For this reason the
field is dominated by the
design of a niche, or
mihrab, usually arched in
some way, inside which the
faithful kneels, resting his
head on the top of the arch
and his hands on the
corners. Prayer-rug designs
are associated with
Anatolia and date to the
15th century, but prayer
rugs have become

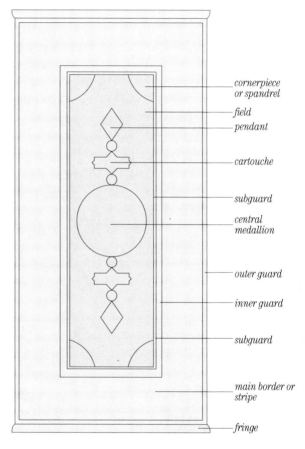

cornerpiece
or spandrel

field

pendant

cartouche

subguard

central
medallion

outer guard

inner guard

subguard

main border or
stripe

fringe

widespread throughout the
Orient.

Nondirectional carpets
can be looked at from any
direction. The decoration
of the field is not directed
at any one point and is
formed by continuous
elements, completely
equal self-enclosed motifs
that are repeated so as to
occupy the entire field.
Such full-field decorations
are regular, and the
designs are arranged in
rectangular or diagonal
rows or form grids or

endless repeats. This kind
of layout includes, for
example, carpets with
arabesques, those in which
the decoration is
dominated or formed by a
continuous ribbon
extending with curving or
geometric regularity across
the entire field.

Centralized layouts can
also be looked at from any
direction, but their
decoration is based on a
central, dominant element
around which secondary
motifs are arranged. The

central element is usually a medallion, a variously shaped rosette—circular, ogival, starlike, or sharply polygonal—that often ends in two small, usually drop-shaped, pendants. Medallion layouts are the most widespread and best known among antique carpets and can be disposed in various ways. The field is usually dominated by a single, central, more or less large medallion accompanied by fractions of four other secondary medallions set in the corners of the carpet. In the so-called four-and-one arrangement, the four secondary medallions are presented whole and are arranged near the corners as though wheeling around the central medallion. In another variation, known as the superimposed-medallions layout, a row of two or more medallions extends the length of the field; the medallions can be of the same size, the central one can be larger and the lateral ones smaller, and vice versa.

All these layouts are quite old, the most recent having come into existence during the 16th to 17th centuries. Codified by tradition, they have become classic and provide the basis of modern-day carpet design. Directional, nondirectional, and centralized layouts provide the frameworks on which designs and the selection of decorative motif are based.

21

DECORATION
AND STYLE

Left: Shirvan medallion carpet; Caucasus, 19th century. Right: Tabriz medallion carpet; Persia, 19th century. These examples demonstrate two ways of interpreting the same layout, the first in the geometric style, the second in the floral, or curvilinear.

Design and carpet style

The design of a carpet is identified by the way in which the layout and decorative motifs are interpreted and articulated. The methods of doing so are many and vary according to geographical area and place of production. Even so, all designs are expressed following two general primary languages: geometric style and floral style. The distinction between the two styles is based on the type of line used: the first uses straight lines—horizontal, vertical, and diagonal segments—to form its various elements, while the second uses curved lines, for which reason it is also called the curvilinear style.

The geometric style is usually (though this is not a rule) made using symmetrical knots, for their regular shape makes them better suited to forming straight lines, and it leads to the creation of abstract or stylized figures distributed with measured equilibrium across the area of the carpet. Geometric-style carpets have an immediate, elementary, and sometimes primitive character, which in most cases reflects a simplified organization of the work; in fact, the geometric style is primarily the style of small artisans, as well as the style used by most nomadic populations, for aside from using a horizontal loom, such peoples usually hand down their carpet designs orally from generation to generation. The geometric style is widespread but is most concentrated in Anatolia, the Caucasus, and central Asia.

The floral, or curvilinear, style was probably born at the end of the 15th century and was further developed in Persia during the 1500s. It usually makes use of asymmetrical knots (but, again, this is not a rule), for being smaller and irregular in form, they are better suited to reproducing even

Left: Shirvan prayer rug; Caucasus, 19th century.
Right: Kashan prayer rug; Persia, 19th century. Like the examples opposite, these show different stylistic

interpretations of the same layout, one geometric and the other floral.

the finest curved lines. This style creates complicated designs of floral or arabesqued elements, more or less naturalistic, in which the figures of men and animals often appear. Such carpets have a complex, detailed character, the fruit of an equally complex work organization in which the planning was done by a separate figure, the master designer (*ustad* in Persian), and only the actual work remained in the hands of the weaver. The birth of this style marked the separation of the carpet-making process into two stages, planning and execution, and also brought about the introduction of cartoons as models. As for

geographical distribution, the floral style is considered the highest expression of Persian carpets.

Style and production area

Using the geometric or floral language, designs and decorative motifs have been composed, interpreted, and translated by colours following procedures that vary so much from epoch to epoch and place to place— and even within single geographical areas—that no broad, regular stylistic classification without exceptions could ever be formulated. Even so, bearing in mind that every carpet is the fruit of the relationship

among technique, history, tradition, and function and that its overall character is determined by the context in which it was made, one can establish four broad stylistic groups, which correspond to the four cultural spheres that have taken shape and evolved over the centuries. These are the nomadic tribe, the small village workshop, the specialized city workshop, and the large court atelier.

Carpet production is a fundamental activity for tribal nomads and an essential part of their lives— carpets are not made simply to earn money. Using rudimentary horizontal looms, easily dismantled and

Luri carpet with stylized floral decoration; Persia, end 19th century. A characteristic example of the carpets made by Persian nomads.

portable, even once work has begun on a carpet, women create small carpets (averaging 30-45 x 60-80 inches), often narrow in shape, decorated with abstract or stylized geometric designs following patterns codified by each tribe's tradition and handed down orally. The number of colours employed is usually few, and the colours can be either bright or quite dark but are, in general, strongly contrasting. The tribal carpet seems animated by an ingenuous and spontaneous spirit, naif, but overtly full of pride and boldness, aspects that add to its attraction.

The other three production spheres involve settled peoples who, having no need to move and being able to use the walls and ceilings of their houses as supporting elements, have adopted the largest and most evolved vertical looms. Small village workshops are not above making occasional use of horizontal looms and are usually run by the women of a single family nucleus who make carpets for their own use and for small-scale commerce. Their carpets are relatively small, like those of nomads, but their designs are more various, open to external influences and invention and thus not based only on oral tradition. Abstract or stylized forms dominate, and the colours

Below: Detail of a
Tekke carpet with
typical geometric
decoration; western
Turkestan, 19th
century.
Bottom: Kerman
medallion carpet;
Persia, 19th century.

The Luri (opposite)
and Tekke carpets
were made by
nomads; this, more
refined example, was
made in a specialized
city workshop.

are more numerous and varied than in carpets made by nomads; the general character is more evolved and balanced.

Specialized city workshops use only vertical looms and produce medium and large carpets (averaging 60-80 x 85-100 inches). They make carpets for sale only, both at local markets and for export abroad, and employ many labourers. The fundamental difference between these workshops and nomadic tribes and village workshops, however, is that at the city workshops the weaver does not create the design; he only executes the designs of the *ustad*, the master who creates the

cartoons, or models. The presentations are complex and worked out using a great variety of designs, for the most part adopting the curvilinear style, accompanièd by the use of many perfectly-balanced colours. Carpets created in this way, with great care given every part, have an elaborate and refined spirit.

Court ateliers are a special sphere of the past. Their creations were made for emperors and shahs and include unique pieces, some of enormous size (the Ardebil carpet is 34 feet 6 inches x 17 feet 6 inches), that were planned by the most important court artists, who created highly refined designs using the most elaborate curvilinear styles. These carpets include incredible abstract and figurative forms, presented in a vast range of colours and sometimes enriched by precious silver and gold threads. The character that emerges from these rare carpets, most of which are preserved in museums and some of which were signed by the artists involved, is highly refined and exclusive, perfectly suited to sumptuous court palaces.

One might assume from this overview that carpets produced by city workshops or court ateliers were the most valuable. In reality, each sphere has its works of great value and appeal.

Tribal carpets, for example, have always had the merit of reflecting a culture uncontaminated by commercial demands.

The historical-stylistic development of carpets

A discussion of the four spheres of production can be used to trace a brief overview of the historical-stylistic development of the Oriental carpet; further information will come to light during the examination of each specific geographic area.

As indicated by the ancient Pazyryk carpet, the first designs used on carpets were evidently in the geometric style and used simple abstract or stylized forms. To these formulas were later added totemic or heraldic elements, though new elements were always anchored to ancient formulas.

The geometric style was highly developed in Anatolia from the 11th to 13th centuries under the Seljuk dynasty and dominated carpet style unopposed— only dividing itself into abstract and stylized forms—until the end of the 15th century, when a new language, the curvilinear, began to spread. The introduction of the curvilinear style was stimulated in part by new floral designs recently introduced from China, such as the "cloudband" pattern,

mythical animals, and naturalistic flowers inspired by the peony and lotus flower. Elaborated in the great court workshops of the Ottoman emperors and particularly in the highly-organized Persian ateliers of the Safavid shahs, this new style underwent enormous development in the 16th century, thanks in part to the involvement of the period's leading artists. Carpets began to fill with highly complicated floral and figurative designs, sometimes of a naturalistic character, and the layouts were varied or altered with new methods, such as the much used medallion layout, without doubt the leader of this classical epoch. Amid this great creative ferment the stylistic differences between the two leading "homelands" of the Oriental carpet grew more marked: Anatolia preferred to continue with its geometric tradition, while Persia made the floral style its own. The first Indian carpets appeared during the 16th century, a result of the express wishes of the Mogul emperors. These highly individual carpets were distinguished by extremely naturalistic floral designs inspired by Western herbals. There were no important innovations in Persia, Anatolia, and India during the next centuries; classical formulas continued to provide the sources of

inspiration and were repeated, initially with a certain expressive energy. The productions of the Caucasus and Turkestan, impervious to the new styles, remained faithful to their own traditional geometric language. China, without an ancient carpet tradition, followed its own particular styles, characterized by geometric and floral designs, for the most part symbolic. In Europe, carpets had been made in Spain since the 12th century, and to these were added the great French carpets of Aubusson and Savonnerie during the 17th century and English carpets during the 18th.

At the end of the 18th century the increasing cultural and political contacts between the West and East led to the first appearance of Western influences in Oriental carpets. The first effect of these influences was a change in the dyes toward pastel tones, but Western influence culminated in Anatolia during the first half of the 19th century in the Majid style, also called the Turkish baroque, which was characterized by the introduction of such Frenchified decorative elements as naturalistic flowers and grape vines.

DECORATION AND STYLE

The 19th century marked the beginning of the subjection of the art of carpets to commercial rule, beginning with the introduction of chemical dyes and leading to the increasingly exhausted repetition of classical layouts accompanied by growing rigidity in the traditional designs. Modern production represents the debasement of those formulas, which have been jumbled together and are repeated as from a frozen repertory. Although still made with great technical skill, carpets are for the most part no longer interpretations of vital and spontaneous expressions, but are produced in response to the dictates of the market. This is not true of tribal production, which has remained isolated and enclosed within its own expressive sphere composed of designs that are simple but ancient and spontaneous.

Decorations and symbols

In addition to the fundamental, practical function that we have emphasized, the carpet also has a profound symbolic meaning in the Orient. It represents a special, magical space. Its borders form the terrestrial sphere, the realm of mankind, and serve as a walled barrier protecting the field, which represents the universe, the celestial sphere, the divine. At one time, carpet decoration was designed to be perfectly suitable for such a space and included elements of a spontaneous ornamental character as well as elements of an eminently symbolic character.

With historical-cultural changes and the passing of centuries, many symbolic decorative motifs lost their original meanings and shapes and were transformed into simple abstract elements. For example, many heraldic totems and shields of ancient tribal origin have been transformed into simple polygonal medallions. Other symbolic decorations have maintained their forms and can still be recognized, even if over time their appearance on carpets has lost its meaning, and they have assumed an exclusively ornamental character.

Apart from the decorative motifs of China, which

constitute a separate
subject, in order to
understand and recognize
the decorative elements
used in carpets, especially
elements that appear in the
production of many areas
and are thus the fruits of
ancient common religions
and cultures, they must be
traced back to their original
meaning, which means
turning to the sphere of
Islamic culture and, beyond,
to pre-Islamic religions,
such as shamanism and
Buddhism. The shamanistic
conception of the forces of
nature as the seat of good
and evil and the later faith
in a divinity that can be
neither depicted nor
defined, from Islam,
constitute the theoretical
background to the creation
of these decorations, to
which must be added the
contribution of certain

symbolic Buddhist elements
that arrived from the Far
East. The principal
decorations are the
following.

The tree. The tree is among
the most common
decorations on Oriental
carpets, where it appears
either multiplied to form the
garden layout or alone and
larger, as in the carpets

typical of eastern Turkestan
made between the 17th and
19th centuries. In both
stylized or naturalistic forms,
the tree appears in almost all
production areas because its
symbolic value was
recognized throughout the
Orient. It represents the
"tree of life," symbol of
fertility and continuity, and
also the "axis of the world,"

DECORATION AND STYLE

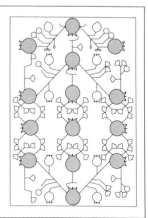

symbol of the connection between the underground roots (the world of magic), the earth (the human world), and the divine with its branches (the celestial world). In this sense it is often represented inside the mihrab of prayer rugs. Sometimes it is flanked by pairs of birds, an allusion to union and regeneration. The legendary waq-waq tree is of Indian origin. Its branches and fruits are transformed into the heads of monstrous men and animals screaming "waq-waq," hence its name. This motif, which alludes to the energy bursting out of the tree, but also to its divinatory powers, appears on Indian carpets of the 16th century and later on Safavid and 19th-century Persian carpets. The place of the tree is often taken by flowers and plants growing from a vase, which have the same meaning.

Clouds. Clouds are symbolized by the "cloud collar," a Chinese motif composed of a circle with four or more elements shaped like multifoil arrows that create a clover. The cloud motif alludes to the concept of the "gate of heaven," a celestial entryway for communication with and protection from the divine, just as clouds surround and protect the sun. The "cloud collar," simplified in the form of the "cloudband," has been used in Anatolian and Persian

1-2. Two versions of the "cloud collar."
3. The "cloudband" motif derived from the "cloud collar."
4. The "trefoil" motif derived from a stylization of the "cloud collar."

5. The chintamani *motif, also known as "thunder and lightning."*
Bottom: Detail of a Ushak carpet with chintamani *motifs, Anatolia, 17th century.*

carpets since the 16th century, and as the "clover" motif it was used in ancient Caucasian and most of all eastern Turkoman carpets. The "cloudband" is a transformation of a single point of the "collar" into a winding bandlike motif resembling the Greek letter omega that is called *chi*; it is used in the field of carpets but more often in the border. The "clover" motif is a linear, stylized version of the "collar" transformed into a row of elements resembling lilies or clovers that is pierced by an identical reversed row of a different colour; it is used only in the borders of carpets. In borders, both the "cloudband" and "clover" motif originally emphasized the meaning of "door to the heavens," of protection of the divine, represented by the field. Another motif connected to clouds is the *chintamani*, also called "thunder and lightning," found as a full-field element in some 16th-century Anatolian carpets. It consists of two small wavy lines beneath three small disks arranged to form a triangle. Its origin is unclear: it may be a reworking of Tamerlane's coat-of-arms or it may be based on an ancient Buddhist symbol, but it seems most probable that it is an imitation of the spotted skins of such animals as leopards used by

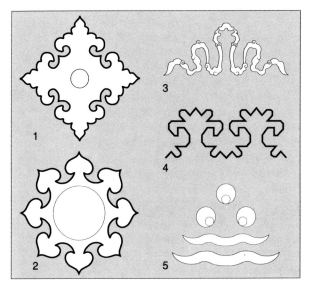

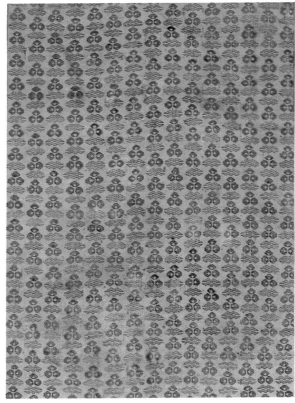

31

DECORATION
AND STYLE

Below: Diagram of superimposed-medallions motif from a 19th-century Caucasian Shirvan carpet.

Bottom: Diagram of three different medallions with pendants, typical of Persian carpets. From the left: Concentric circle, round polylobate; ogival polylobate.

shamans during their sacred rites.

Central medallion. Protected by the borders and located in the center of the field, the medallion represents the divine sun, the state nearest the level of the supernatural. This meaning is symbolized both in the geometric versions with polygonal medallions arranged in the "four-and-one" layout, frequent in Anatolia and the Caucasus, and in the Persian curvilinear versions with round or ogival polygonal medallions that terminate with two pendants (the sun and moon) and are accompanied by four corner motifs. In both cases, the four secondary elements

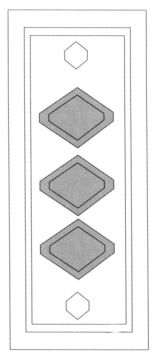

serve to reinforce the symbolism, representing the "solar gates" for nearing heaven, while protecting the center.

Superimposed medallions. The superimposed-medallions layout is thought to be derived from Buddhist symbolism and to represent the Buddha, Sakyamuni, seated between his two acolytes; for this reason, the central medallion differs in size and ornamentation from the outer two. Frequent in the Caucasus and Anatolia in polygonal forms, the layout was much used in eastern Turkestan, where it was characterized by round medallions.

Prayer rugs. Prayer rugs are the Islamic rug type *par*

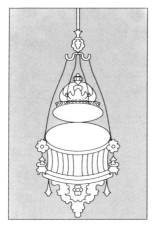

excellence at both the symbolic and practical levels. The faithful Muslim can prostrate himself in prayer on any carpet, but once chosen, the carpet used for prayer must be used exclusively for that purpose. The niche, or mihrab, has the practical function of orienting the faithful toward Mecca and is based on the niche facing Mecca located in the internal wall of every mosque, the form of which it reproduces in a more or less schematic way. It therefore represents the "archway to paradise," the entrance to understanding and paradise, to be attained through daily prayer. At the same time, the mihrab forms a refuge, a place that protects the faithful and puts him in contact with the divine. The interior of this sacred place is often decorated with the "tree of life" or a flowering vase and has an area for the water basins used in ritual ablutions, alluding to the water of eternal life, and from the top of the arch hangs the lamp of the mosque, symbol of Allah and divine light. In some Caucasian and tribal Persian productions hands are presented in the corners, one on each side; these have been variously interpreted as the hands of Fatima, daughter of Muhammad, an allusion to the five Islamic rules, as a contraction of the name Allah written in Arabic, or, more simply, as a suggestion for the position in which to place the hands during prayer. The prayer rug, born in Anatolia in the 15th century, spread throughout all of the Islamic East, but Anatolia remained the production area most dedicated to it.

The garden. In every culture, Eastern or Western, the idea of the garden is

DECORATION
AND STYLE

connected to the concept of paradise. Indeed, the word *paradise* is derived from the Persian *pairideieza*, meaning "garden, enclosure, park." In Islam, the idealized garden in which everything flowers and the four rivers of life flow represents the final goal of the faithful. To present this theme, 17th-century Persian artists took their inspiration from an idealized view of the shah's gardens, which were divided in rectangular or square areas by canals of water. This led to the garden layout, a regular composition of lawns with trees, flower beds, and often

animals. The decoration was applied most frequently in Kerman and in Kurdistan, but it was widespread in the India of the Mogul court, whose carpets are distinguished by their greater naturalism. The Ottoman court remained indifferent to the style, for the more orthodox sentiments of the Sunni were stronger in Anatolia.

The human figure. The human figure is absolutely without symbolic meaning in Oriental carpets: It could not be otherwise within the sphere of an iconoclastic culture like Islam. In fact, the *Sunna*, the collection of moral sayings and

anecdotes of Muhammad, forbids every figurative expression, since such expressions might lead to idolatry and in themselves constitute an outrage as they imitate divine creation. The Anatolian artists at the Ottoman court, being Sunni and thus more orthodox, remained faithful to this precept; the same was not true of the Persian artists at the Safavid court, who were Shiites and less rigid on this point. According to their beliefs, figurative art could be adopted as long as it was directed toward the spiritual or contemplative. For this reason figures of humans and animals began

to appear in 16th-century Persian carpets and later in those of India. These figures were shown in a naturalistic way but were used exclusively to render the idea of paradise or to reflect moral concepts by way of epic or mythical episodes, as was done in the highly developed miniatures of the same period. Men appear in hunting carpets, but they have no particular meaning and never perform leading roles in the decorative economy of the carpet, and even when they appear in epic scenes, the intent is absolutely not naturalistic, but moral. In the same way, each animal in an animal carpet has no value in itself but is part of the context created to render an idealized universe and is equal to the flowers or arabesques past which it moves.

Hunting. Hunting was a popular activity in the Orient, a symbol of dexterity, strength, and domination over nature. Reserved almost exclusively to the rulers and their courts, hunting, like the garden theme, also had a meaning connected to the idea of paradise and thus with spiritual activities. Hunting carpets in which scenes of armed horsemen and prey spread across a field full of arabesques and floral elements were created at the Safavid Persian court, with most of the production in Isfahan. They were later imitated in a more naturalistic style by Indian artists at the Mogul court.

Animals. The animals in carpets can be real or fantastic. Such real "noble" animals as deer, horses, and leopards often appear battling one another against floral backgrounds in the Safavid Persian carpets called animal carpets, and domestic animals appear in tribal carpets, but always as secondary, stylized

Below: Kashan animal carpet; Persia, 19th century. Such "noble" animals as gazelles are shown in a curvilinear style.

Bottom: Diagram of domestic animals as they appear in nomad and village carpets:1. dog; 2. cock; 3. camel; 4. dromedary; 5. peacock; 6. dove.

elements. Both real and fantastic animals appear in scenes of animal battles. These battles represent the inevitable struggle between good and evil, whether on earth or in the cosmos, thus symbolizing the balance of creation. Of Chinese origin, this theme spread to central Asia between the 14th and 15th centuries. Also of ancient Chinese origin are two fantastic animals, the dragon, symbol of omnipotence, and the phoenix, symbol of immortality; when paired, they represent the matrimonial union, while doing battle they allude to cosmic balance and harmony. These fantastic animals spread westward around the 14th-15th centuries, inspiring, for example, ancient Caucasian dragon carpets.

Arabesques. A decorative element common to all Islamic arts, the arabesque is a perfect expression of the iconoclastic Muslim spirit since it permits decoration without figurative representation. Its continuous rhythm, endlessly repeatable, facilitates contemplation, and its abstract forms avoid the temptation to idolatry. The arabesque is a ribbon without beginning or end, and nor can it have them since it expresses the search for the divine, for that which is truly

limitless. At the same time, like a magic tent, it reveals the dimension of the divine that is beyond itself, while continuing to hide it. Furthermore, its characteristics of continuity and repetition are well suited to the *horror vacui* typical of the Islamic spirit, that distrust and anguish at empty spaces or those occupied by only a few rigorously ordered elements. In carpet decorations, the arabesque is placed, because of its importance, in the field, and appears in two versions. The first is geometric and consists of a large ribbon regularly articulated by corners and plaits, typical of the ancient production of Ushak, a town in western Anatolia. The second version is curvilinear and takes advantage of the branches of various floral elements to wind among them, creating an intricate play of thin, curved, and sinuous lines. Difficult to create, this version was popular in Persia during the 16th century and represents one of the fundamental bases of the new curvilinear style.

Decorative motifs

The decoration of Oriental carpets includes a myriad of extremely various ornamental elements. One group consists of small geometric figures, such as

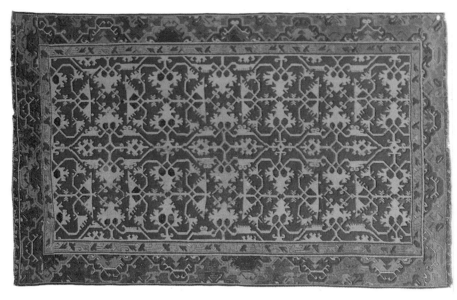

eight-pointed stars, octagons, swastikas, crosses, concentric polygons, S designs, and hooked lozenges. These can appear randomly at any place in a carpet for their primary functions are to fill in open spaces and serve as ornaments to the principal elements. Such elements are, of course, characteristic of production areas using the geometric style, such as those in Anatolia, the Caucasus, Turkestan, and several areas in Persia.

Another numerous group of decorative elements is composed of leaves and flowers. The leaves are usually in a slightly curving lanceolate form, with the outline either smooth or serrated. Flowers, on the other

hand, are far more various and have been interpreted in different ways in different production zones. They have always, however, been divided into two principal types: the rosette, with an oval or roundish shape, symmetrical and usually embellished with petals; and the palmette, the true protagonist of Persian decorations since the 16th century. Of ancient origin, it consists of a pointed flower shaped something like a fan, artichoke, bud, vine leaf, or so on, according to the many varied interpretations; during the 17th century, for example, a particularly rich and elaborate version was created in Persia and called the Shah Abbas in honor of that period's ruler.

The palmette was used on all areas of carpets, and in compositions can either share importance with the primary element, as in the *herati* design, or be itself the principal element, as in the in-and-out palmette motif. The lotus and peony appear on Chinese carpets, and flowers of all kinds, rendered with extreme naturalism, have distinguished carpets from the Indian court since the 16th century.

Yet another group of ornamental elements in carpet design is composed of very particular decorative motifs. While some of these motifs have more than one place of origin (in some cases several areas quite distant one from another), and though they were

Diagrams of decorative motifs with floral origins. 1. rosette; 2-6. palmettes in variously curvilinear versions; 7-9. boteh in the geometric, floral, and "mother-and-son" versions.

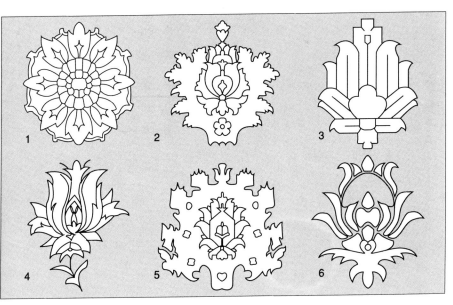

interpreted in various ways, they can be identified and equated nonetheless. Other motifs, on the contrary, are the distinguishing characteristic of a single geographic zone. Appearing as both single or repeating elements, and in geometric or curvilinear style, these decorative motifs have been divided into two broad groups based on where they are usually used in carpets: field motifs and border motifs.

Field motifs

Field motifs can constitute the single, or full-field, decoration of the field, repeated in parallel rows, presented specularly, or arranged in some other way to cover the area; or they can appear together with other decorative elements, whether larger (medallions) or smaller (rosettes, eight-pointed stars, swastikas). The principal field motifs, those most often used, include the following.

Boteh. The *boteh* and *herati* designs are the most common motifs in the Orient, but without doubt the *boteh* is the decorative element best known in the West because it has been familiarized through textiles from India and Kashmir (it is used on Kashmir shawls and is the primary motif of paisley designs), which is why it is sometimes incorrectly referred to as the "Kashmir design." It is usually small in size and because of its shape was once known as the Persian

Hila carpet with three medallions, Caucasus, 19th century. The blue field is spread with geometric multicolour boteh.

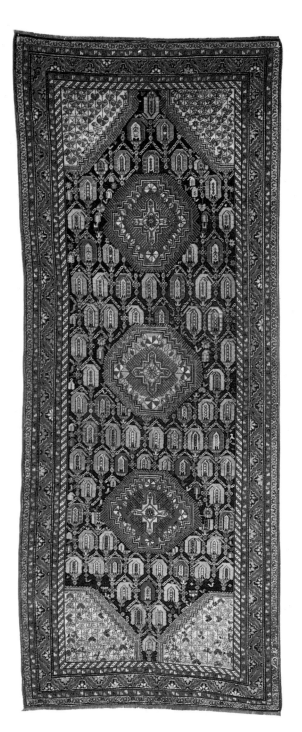

pine pattern. Strange sources of inspiration have been attributed to its shape, which is vaguely similar to a pine cone, teardrop, or cypress leaf with the point bent to one side. It is variously said to be a stylized representation of an almond, the sacred flame of the Zoroastrian religion, the tear of Buddha, a feather, a cypress tree, even the imprint of a closed fist on a mud or plaster surface. In reality, although its origins are obscure, the fact that its name is derived from a Persian word meaning "cluster of leaves" would indicate that its source of inspiration must have come from the floral world. Translated in geometric or curvilinear forms, it is usually multiplied and arranged in parallel rows to cover the entire field, but it also appears alone as a complement to other decorative elements. It first appeared in carpets during the 18th century and during the 19th successfully spread through Persia, as well as Anatolia and the Caucasus. It is also used as a border motif.

Herati. Like the *boteh*, the *herati* design is widespread throughout the Orient, but it is more ancient, having been developed in 16th-century Persia during the magnificent Safavid dynasty. It is named for its probable place of origin, the town of Herat (part of

Below: Diagram of the herati motif. Around the central rhomboidal element are long curving leaves. Because the leaves resemble small fish the motif is also known in Persia as rize mahi, or "small fish."
Bottom: Detail of a Senneh carpet with full-field herati decoration; Persia, 19th century.

Persia until the second half of the 19th century, when it passed to Afghanistan), where carpets with similar designs were made during very early times.

Interpreted in versions so various that it is sometimes difficult to recognize, the *herati* consists of a complex play of floral elements: four flowers (usually palmettes) are located at the points of a diamond element, often formed of their stalks; inside the diamond is a small, round flower, while outside it are four outwardly curling leaves. Because these narrow, elongated leaves resemble small fish, the motif is also known as *mahi*, from the Persian word for "fish." The *herati*

design often appears as the single decorative element in carpets, multiplied in orderly rows across the entire field, or it is employed with other decorations in medallion layouts. Born in

curvilinear style, the *herati* has been interpreted in many ways, both geometric and naturalistic, and is, in fact, the motif most subject to transformation. Since the 16th century it has been most popular in Persia, especially in the towns of Herat and Isfahan. It is also used as a border motif.

Gul. The *gul* consists of a small octagonal, hexagonal, or rhomboidal medallion that is variously shaped (rectilinear, multifoil, hooked, serrated, etc.) and subdivided in four parts of different colours inside which are other small geometric figures, such as eight-pointed stars, squares, lozenges, and rectangles, all variously decorated. The

Left: Diagrams of
various gul
medallions; such guls
characterize the
carpets of western
Turkestan.

Right: Detail of a
Tekke carpet with
guls; western
Turkestan, 19th
century.

origin of this motif is
unknown, and its peculiar
design has spawned the
most various
interpretations, from a rose
to an elephant foot to that of
a camel. The name *gul* is
derived from Persian and
means "flower," which might
make one think of a plant
origin, but the design may
also be derived from ancient
tribal emblems. There is no
uncertainty about its

resemblance to the four-part
octagonal medallions that
typify ancient productions of
Anatolia and the Caucasus.
The *gul* is the distinctive
motif of the production of
western Turkestan, where it
was used as a full-field
motif, multiplied in parallel
rows and alternated with
secondary, polygonal or
cruciform, decorative
motifs. Incorrectly called
the Bukhara design, after

the name of the city where
rugs were collected and
marketed but not made, the
gul changes form, as will be
seen, and at times also its
name, according to which
Turkoman tribe employed it.
Cloudband. This motif, of
ancient Chinese origin,
consists of a twisting band,
shaped something like the
Greek letter omega, called a
chi ; its width and windings
vary from version to version.

As a field motif, it appears in repetitions or arranged in various ways, but always together with various decorative floral elements, such as palmettes and arabesques, mixing in with them and standing out only when its size increases. It can be found in 16th-century Persian floral carpets (especially from Herat) and Indian carpets, and was later used as a field decoration in carpets from both of those areas. It is used most often, however, as a border motif.

Chintamani . This ancient symbolic motif is composed of two small wavy lines beneath three small disks arranged to form a triangle. It is used as a field motif in repeated offset rows that usually determine a directional reading of the design. Usually dark on a light background, its name is applied to a particular kind of antique carpet made in Ushak in Anatolia.

In-and-out palmette . This motif relates to carpets with floral designs in which two pairs of palmettes form the ornamental motif, their tops alternately directed toward the interior and exterior of the carpet. Usually arranged across the full field, they are completed by other,

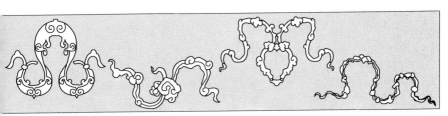

DECORATION
AND STYLE

Below: Diagram of the chintamani *decoration full field.*

Bottom: Diagram of three designs based on the harshang *motif: a zoomorphic palmette; a rhomboidal flower with forked leaves; a round flower similar to a toothed wheel.*

secondary, elements, such as cloudbands and arabesques. This motif was created in Persia during the 16th century and enjoyed much popularity; it was repeated in later centuries in less articulated versions, stripped of its surrounding elements.

Harshang or kharshang. This complex motif, usually arranged in parallel rows across the full field, is composed of three principal elements: a characteristic "flaming halo" palmette; a certain rhomboidal flower arranged diagonally, from which spread four rectilinear stalks, each ending in a branching plant element; and another round flower, similar to a toothed wheel. The name *harshang* (from the Persian for "crab") refers to the vaguely zoomorphic form of the characteristic palmette. This motif, probably derived from 16th-century Persian designs, developed in the 18th century in northern Persia (Kurdistan and Azerbaijan) and in the Caucasus. Over time, as can be seen mostly through 19th-century examples, its complex design disappeared, and in most later carpets only two, or even one, of the elements remain. Its geometric version became characteristic of the carpets from several Caucasian production areas, such as Kuba and Baku.

Afshan or avshan. Very

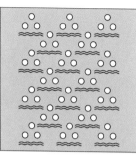

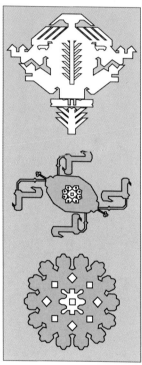

similar to the *harshang*, this motif is distinguished by its greater simplicity. Always arranged in parallel rows, it alternates rosettes and pairs of palmettes; from the ends of the palmettes spread branching plant elements, wheeling around a small flower. Derived from the same 16th-century

prototype as the harshang, the Afshan was developed in the 18th century between northern Persia and the Caucasus; it was employed to a great extent in the Caucasus during the 19th century in increasingly geometric and enlarged versions, particularly visible in carpets from the areas of Kuba and Baku.

Mina khani. This motif consists of four identical flowers, round and petalled, similar to daisies, attached to one another by thin shoots to form a curvilinear diamond lattice inside which is another, smaller flower. Repeated across the entire field, this composition creates a sort of grid structure. The motif was developed in 18th-century Persia and was based on a 16th-century prototype. Its area of origin is unknown, though debated to be between Kurdistan and Khorasan. Its name is no help, since *mina* is a woman's name in Persian that has been interpreted as also being the name of the flower used in the composition (some even hold, erroneously, that the motif should be limited to the flower only); furthermore, since *khaneh* means "house," *mina khani* could indicate the garden of a house. During the 19th century this motif became the characteristic element of carpets from the Persian city of Veramin.

Below left: Detail of a Kuba carpet with floral decoration; Caucasus, 17th century. Visible are Afshan motifs with their typical forking elements.

Below right: Diagrams of Afshan and mina khani *motifs.*

Bottom: Veramin carpet with floral decoration; Persia, modern workmanship. This carpet repeats the traditional design of the area with the typical mina khani *motif arranged full field.*

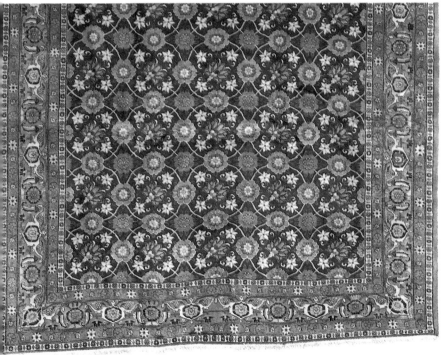

45

*Diagram of the
Persian zel-i-sultan
motif, which is formed
of a central vase with
flowers flanked by two
birds.*

*Zel-i-sultan or zellol
sultan.* This motif is easy to
recognize even though it
has been made in versions
of varying degrees of
naturalism. It is composed
of a flowering vase flanked
by two birds; the design is
usually repeated across the
entire field of the carpet.
Closely related to the
ancient motif consisting of a
tree flanked by two birds,
the zel-i-sultan seems to
have been made first in
Persia during the 19th
century for a member of the
court, since its name means
"shadow of the sultan"; the
name might refer to the
hereditary prince Zellol of
the Qajar dynasty (1786-
1925), or to one of the
sultan's counselors.
Whatever its precise area of
origin, the motif, which
dates without doubt to the
19th century, spread
through Persia, seeing
particular use in the
Malayer region.

Border motifs

In no sense should border
motifs be considered as
secondary to field motifs, for
not just complementary to
the decoration of carpets,
their design and colours
determine its final balance.
Furthermore, being less
subject to cultural changes
and stylistic trends than
field motifs, border motifs
often offer solid help in the
identification and dating of
specimens.

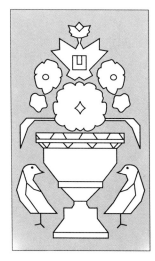

The outer areas of
Oriental carpets can be
broken down into
numerous borders (seven
is considered the perfect
number), which are
divided into main borders
(or stripes), large and
usually unbroken, and
narrower and more
numerous minor borders
(or guards). The
decorative motifs used in
borders are numerous and
varied; among the most
common are tendrils, S
shapes, rosettes, swastikas,
frets, and flowers. The most
important symbolically are
the following.
    Boteh. Boteh border
motifs are identical to
boteh field motifs and are
equally common in carpet
decoration. *Boteh* motifs
usually appear as a single
decorative motif in minor
borders, repeated in series
to form a single row. In
main borders, *boteh* motifs

usually appear together
with other motifs, both
primary and secondary. The
shape of the *boteh* changes,
becoming more or less
geometric or curvilinear,
according to the
production area.
    Herati. Herati border
motifs are less articulated
than *herati* field motifs and
involve basic elements
repeated in rows, usually a
single palmette alternating
with a single rosette
divided by the typical
curling leaves. The versions
are so numerous and varied
that recognizing this border
motif is sometimes
difficult. It was born in
Persia during the 16th
century, where it enjoyed
such popularity that it
became virtually an
emblem of that region;
during the 19th century it
was rendered in a new form
known as the "turtle"
version, in which the
palmette is transformed
into a flower that vaguely
resembles that animal.
    Cloudband. The
cloudband motif is used as
a field motif, but its
primary use is in borders,
where it fits its original
symbolic meaning of "cloud
collar" and is thereby
connected to the idea of
protecting the field. When
used in borders, it is almost
always the principal
element, appears in large
sizes, and is repeated
regularly in more or less
geometrical winding rows

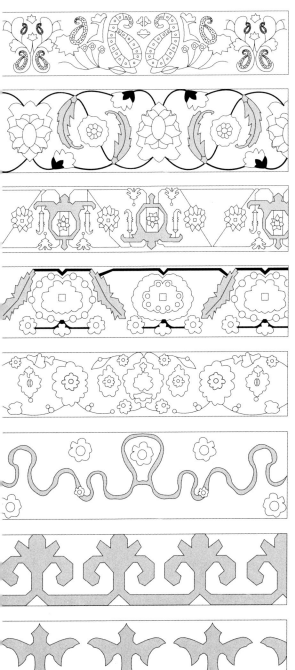

of omegas, all pointing the same way or in opposite directions—internal-external—to the field. This motif was used in the main borders of carpets from the town of Ushak in western Anatolia as early as the 16th century, adding a special character both to those with *chintamani* designs and those with the so-called bird pattern.

Trefoils. Descended from the "cloud collar," this motif is composed of identical units resembling a trefoil or stylized clover arranged in two continuous reciprocal rows (one facing inward, the other outward), defined by the use of contrasting colors (red/yellow; red/blue). The interpretation of this motif varies a great deal according to provenance. Present in ancient carpets from Anatolia, the Caucasus, and eastern Turkestan, the trefoil motif is particularly characteristic of Turkestan carpets, in which it appears in large sizes along the main border.

Medachyl or madakhell. Probably a 19th-century simplification of the trefoil motif, the *medachyl* is also created using two rows of different-colored elements that are opposed and reciprocal, but in this case the design is extremely geometric, being reduced to rows of diamond-shaped arrowheads. Another, even

47

DECORATION AND STYLE

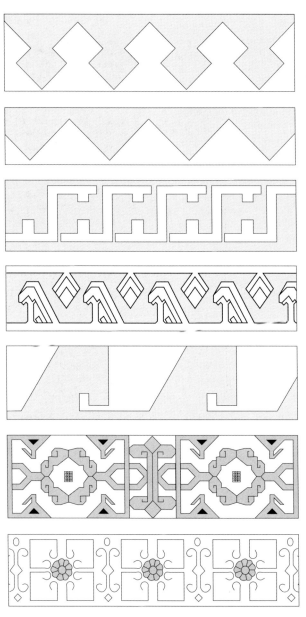

simpler, version of this motif is composed of a series of small triangles in contrasting colors. The *medachyl*, which was used only in minor borders, was reasonably widespread, although it saw most use in carpets of a geometric character, such as those of the Caucasus.

Running dog. This decorative motif probably belongs to the large family of motifs derived from the "cloud collar," since it is composed of two rows of colored specular elements that are reciprocal. Its shape, which varies a great deal according to interpretation, is composed of a series of geometric waves or hooks, more or less large and curved, that have been taken as the heads of dogs. The name has no symbolic or historical meaning. Used mostly to decorate minor borders, it was widespread in Caucasian carpets and was the preferred motif in main borders in the northeastern Caucasus, where it was presented in more elaborate and larger versions.

Kufic or kufesque. Based on the angular shape of the Kufic style of Arabic script adopted by the Seljuk Turks, Kufic motifs are among the most widespread and ancient design motifs; they appear in fragments from Anatolian carpets datable

Diagrams of decorative border motifs. From top to bottom: cartouche motif in the classical Persian version; cartouche motif in the version of antique Transylvanian carpets from Anatolia; cartouche motif in the interpretation of antique Anatolian Lotto examples; cubukli; kotchanak.

to the 13th century. Kufic writing, which is eminently decorative in character, may originally have been applied directly to carpets and then was later transformed into a purely ornamental motif, illegible and without meaning. The motifs are composed of a succession of geometric elements of varying thicknesses. The central, taller element is shaped like a capital I and is flanked by two others, lower and wider, arranged specularly; complementary rosettes are sometimes employed. The size and elaboration vary according to the area of production, and the motif can be found in geometric, closed, or open styles. Usually used in main borders, this motif is found primarily in the production of Anatolia (particularly its antique carpets, such as the Holbeins) and the Caucasus.

Cartouche. This ancient motif is based on the embossed leather covers of the Koran on which a series of sacred verses appeared framed within elongated polygons. Transferred to Persian and Mameluke carpets in the 16th century, the cartouches lost their inscriptions, which were replaced by geometric or floral elements, and became purely decorative motifs; only in prayer rugs did they continue to act as frames for sacred texts. More or less geometric and elongated, sometimes alternating with rosettes, cartouches appear in the main borders of carpets from many production areas; for example, they are a distinguishing characteristic of the borders of the ancient Anatolian carpets known as Transylvanian carpets, which were produced between the first half of the 17th century and the beginning of the 18th.

Cubukli. This motif, widespread in Anatolia, is named for its resemblance to the long, narrow pipes typical of that area. The main border is composed of an assembly of long, narrow continuous stripes (usually seven) in two alternating colors that are enlivened by points or small flowers located at regular distances. Introduced to Anatolia early in the 19th century, this motif enjoyed much success during the second half of that century and came to characterize in particular the carpets of Ghiordes and Kula.

Serrated leaf. This motif is composed of two serrated geometric leaves, arranged

DECORATION AND STYLE

Shirvan carpet with three medallions; Caucasus, 19th century. In the main border (diagram at left) are serrated leaves; medachyls are in the two minor borders. The diagram to the right shows the kotchanak motif.

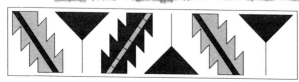

diagonally and separated by a Y-shaped motif that resembles a winecup but is actually a stylized tulip. This basic design is repeated in several colors against the usually lighter background color of the main border. This decoration is characteristic of Caucasian carpets, for example the 19th-century products of Kazak.

Kotchanak. This motif consists of the repetition along the main border of a strange polygon, more or less square or rectangular, open or closed according to the interpretation, and characterized above and below by two pairs of hooks, similar to ram's horns. The interior is decorated with octagons, crosses, or other small geometric elements. This motif distinguishes the carpets of western Turkestan, but appears in several areas of the Caucasus. It may be descended from ancient heraldic totems and is sometimes alternated with other, lesser geometric figures. It sometimes appears in the field, but as widely spaced individual elements.

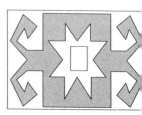

DATING
AND STYLE

◆ Dates, expressed in Islamic numbers or translated into the calendar and characters of the West, sometimes appear in either the border or field of carpets. Such dates should be treated with great caution, for they are not always reliable and were often added by the weaver in an effort to increase a carpet's value. Even so, a working knowledge of dates can be useful. To convert a Muslim year to a year in the Gregorian, or Western, calender, divide the Islamic date by 33.7 (the Muslim calendar is lunar and adds one year to every 33.7 Gregorian, or solar, years); subtract the sum obtained from the date itself; and then add 622, the year of Muhammad's flight to Medina, which marks the beginning of the Islamic era.

Islamic and Arabic Numerals		
Turkish	*Persian*	
٠	٠	0
١	١	1
٢	٢	2
٣	٣	3
٤	٤	4
٥	٥	5
٦	٦	6
٧	٧	7
٨	٨	8
٩	٩	9

In the absence of such relevant information as dates, inscriptions, or even signatures (which are very rare and found only on ancient examples made at court), establishing the date of a carpet is as difficult as ascertaining its identity. The problems begin with the fact that there are not enough antique examples to permit the establishment with any certainty of the chronological development of the designs and motifs of every individual production area. The situation is further complicated by the fact that, in general, one cannot speak of carpet decoration in terms of stylistic periods or particular trends, since the basic models have always been the same: in every production area, the most ancient types became classic motifs that were

n this Caucasian ;arpet (Daghestan) he year of execution, 890, is expressed ollowing both the Western calendar (left) ınd the Islamic (right)

51

Kashan medallion carpet; Persia, 19th century.

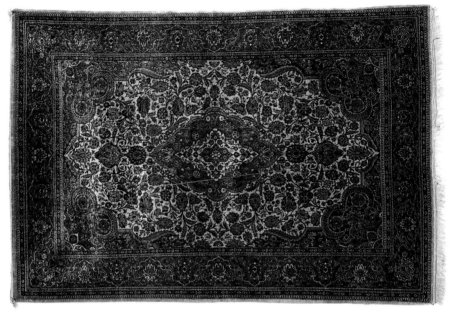

endlessly repeated. A good example of this are the most widespread layouts, those for medallions or prayer rugs.

The process followed when trying to determine the age of a carpet (and such ages are always expressed in relatively broad chronological terms) is much like that used to identify the origin of a carpet and involves close overall examination of the carpet itself. The state of preservation (even if not always a reliable factor) must be considered, along with the technical characteristics (colours obtained using chemical dyes, for example, are certain proof of a manufacture later than 1860-1870) and, most of all, the style. Stylistic analysis

to determine age is conducted by comparing the carpet to examples from the same provenance that are more or less antique or old, taking into consideration the general quality of the design, the type of field and border decorations, and the colour. The quality of the design presents a revealing factor that is both efficacious and immediate. In fact, a clearly drawn and distinct design matched with a harmonious layout, well planned and balanced, including the use of open and filled spaces, usually characterizes the most antique carpets, while a mannered and stiff design, with a layout full of elements distributed following an unbalanced logic, seemingly just to fill space, is typical of more

recent examples.

As for decorative motifs, the purest examples, those in the forms most respected by tradition, can usually be taken as indications of antiquity, while the same motifs transformed into stylized versions, stiffened or exaggerated, reveal more recent manufacture. Some help can be furnished by the presence of a decorative motif known to have appeared at a certain time during a certain period or, vice versa, by the absence of an element known to have disappeared at a certain time.

Colours can also be important in determining age, not only in the technical terms of their organic or artificial nature (whether made by natural or chemical dyes), but also

Below: Kashan medallion carpet; Persia, modern workmanship. Comparison with the example opposite, which has a similar design and colours, reveals how the style has become increasingly rigid and less harmonious. Bottom: Kazak medallion carpet; Caucasus, end 19th century. The colours of this carpet, which are neither strong nor bright, indicate a recent date, sometime from the end of the 19th century onward.

stylistically. The oldest carpets are usually characterized by a large number of strong, brilliant colours, while examples datable from the end of the 18th century onward usually employ a more restricted number colours in a monotonous range, with preference given to light tones, such as pastels.

Finally, one should bear in mind that the 19th century saw the process of degeneration of the indigenous carpet as it was gradually transformed into a commercial product made for exportation and thus designed to meet the demands of the Western marketplace. Therefore carpets made in the Orient during the 19th century, especially after 1860-1870 (following the introduction of chemical dyes), are still products of great value but are usually characterized by designs and colours that show a marked decline in quality from those of the typical and genuine earlier carpets.

THE GEOGRAPHY
OF CARPETS

♦ Decorated following the geometric style or the floral style, tending toward the abstract or the naturalistic, simple or elaborate, the Oriental carpet is composed of an infinity of motifs, designs, and colours. This extremely varying character, combined with the anonymous character of carpets and their highly perishable nature, makes the dating of carpets difficult and renders identification and recognition problematic.

Even so, stylistic and technical analogies have identified seven large basic groups that correspond to seven geographical areas, each of which reveals its own particular character. The examples from within each area are distinguished

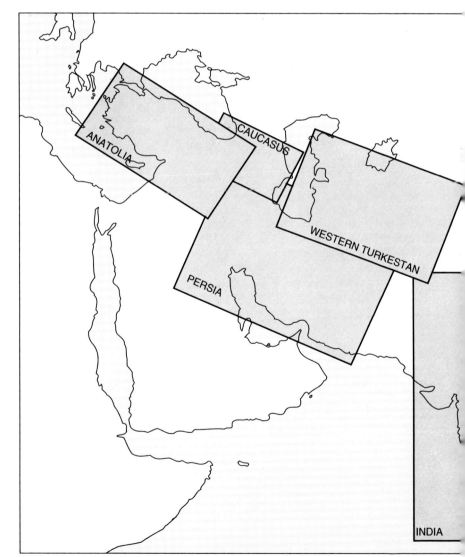

and subdivided further, based in most cases on experimental methods or pure convention, according to their decorative motifs, places of origin, or tribe to which they belonged. The great regions that form the "geography" of the Oriental carpet are Anatolia, the Caucasus, Persia, western Turkestan and eastern Turkestan (central Asia), India, and China. Given such a vast and complex panorama, it is not easy, for example, to distinguish an Anatolian carpet from a Caucasian on the basis of designs and colours. For those who are not experts in the field, the ability to do so represents a big step toward recognizing a mysterious and fascinating artistic creation.

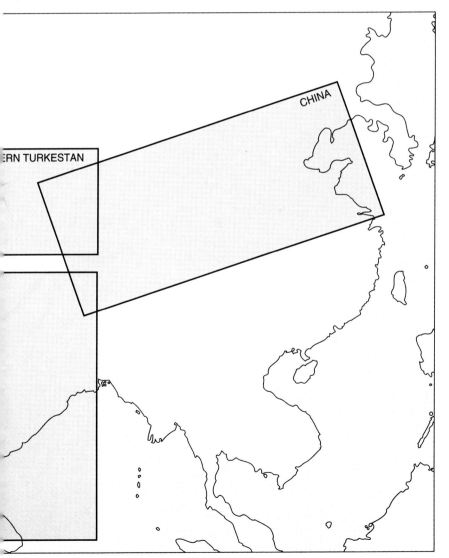

CHINA

ERN TURKESTAN

ANATOLIA

♦ Tied to local tradition and full of religious meaning, Anatolian carpets are distinguished by their fidelity to ancient layouts and designs based on the combination or repetition of simple or complex geometric figures. Even floral elements, when present, are rendered in extremely stylized forms, and human figures and animals are excluded in obedience to the orthodox rules of the Sunnite Muslims. The colours, numerous and lively, are always employed in the strongest tonalities, with a particular taste for sharp contrasts. The predominant colours are red, yellow, blue, and warm shades in general. Technically, all Anatolian carpets (except for certain Hereke examples) are made using the symmetrical knot. The carpets are usually small in size, and the most common shapes are elongated rectangles, although some are decidedly square. The most characteristic type is the prayer rug, variously articulated according to the production center.

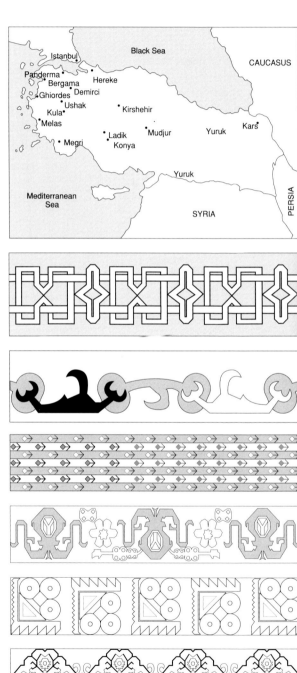

Diagram of the symmetrical, or Ghiordes, knot, typical of Anatolia.

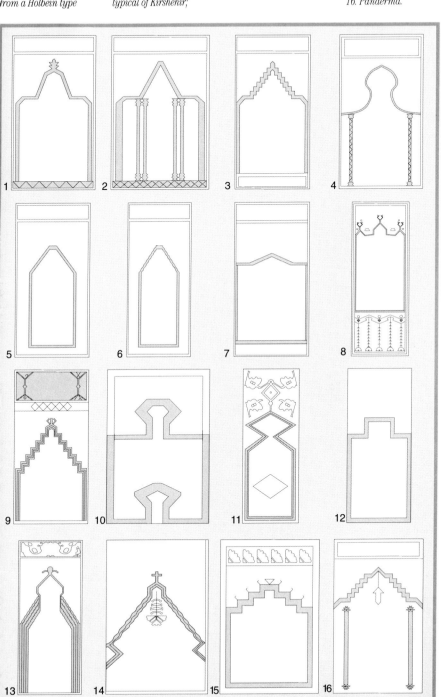

57

ANATOLIA

The birth of a style

The art of the knotted carpet was introduced to Anatolia in the 11th century by the rulers of the Seljuk dynasty, who came from Turkestan and dominated Asia Minor until 1299, imposing on the area their culture and Islamic faith. The study of a group of ancient fragmentary examples, datable to the 13th century and uncovered in central Anatolia at Konya and nearby Beyshehir, has provided background for understanding the Seljuk style. These carpet fragments are made of wool using the symmetrical knot and have full-field decoration: the most common layouts are composed of diagonal or rectangular grids and the endless repetition of various polygons. Eight-pointed stars, hooked octagonals, and borders with Kufic script are the most typical decorative motifs; these elementary motifs, descended from ancient central Asian traditions, were destined to endure many centuries. The predominant colours are various tones of red and dark and light blue. The creation of this group has been attributed to a refined workshop in Konya, ancient capital of the Seljuk state. A separate case is provided by two singular figural carpets of mysterious provenance:

the Berlin, or Ming, carpet and the so-called Marby rug. Both have the same kind of decoration with geometric almost totemic animals (the battle between a dragon and a phoenix in the Berlin carpet; two birds at the sides

of the tree of life in the Marby rug) enclosed within two large rectangles. They have been dated to around the first half of the 15th century and variously connected to Seljuk, Ottoman, and Causasian

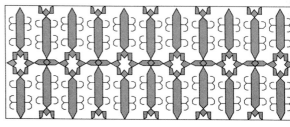

centers as well as to contemporaneous Byzantine textiles, which have similar figural motifs. The Byzantine connection is demonstrated by the fact that, after the Ottoman conquest of Byzantium in 1453, this kind of design disappeared, together with all other representations of animals. The Seljuk models, on the other hand, underwent enormous growth under the new Ottoman dynasty. During their long reign (1299-1922) the Ottomans, who were also Muslims, gave great support to the art of the carpet. The 15th and 16th centuries represent the most splendid period of this production. Only a few examples have survived, but European painting of that period offers us an indirect testimony of these carpets. Oriental carpets, imported exclusively from nearby Anatolia, were common in Europe during that period, and Italian and northern European artists often inserted them in their religious or secular scenes, and the ornamental motifs of these carpets, although reworked, were handed down until the 19th century and later. For this reason, the stylistic classification of Anatolian carpets has come to include certain types that are given the names of the painters who made them famous by reproducing them in their paintings.

Painters and carpets

Holbein carpets, named for
the German painter Hans
Holbein the Younger (1497-
1543), demonstrate the
survival, in reworked forms,
of traditional Seljuk motifs.
The major elements of
these carpets are elegant
geometric medallions, and
the carpets are divided into
two types—small-pattern
Holbeins and large-pattern
Holbeins—according to the
arrangement and size of the
medallions. In the first type,
small octagons, often
including a star, are
arranged in rows across the
field and framed by
characteristic geometric
arabesques that form, in
turn, triangular
interweavings similar to
hearts. Large-pattern
Holbeins have a less
articulated layout that is
based simply on the
composition of two or three
large octagons enclosing
various elements, such as
eight-pointed stars framed
by squares. Both types,
characterized by small
formats and strong colours,
with red and blue
predominating, have
borders decorated in Kufic
script or trefoils. Heirs to
the Seljuk tradition not only
in terms of their decorative
motifs but most of all in
their strong geometric
sensibility, Holbein carpets
enjoyed great success in
later production; beginning
in the 17th century,

Opposite above: Ushak carpet of the small-pattern Holbein type; 16th century. The full-field design of small polygons, often framed by characteristic arabesques, is typical of this area.

Opposite bottom: Detail of a painting by Hans Holbein the Younger in which a large-pattern Holbein carpet appears, recognizable by the two large central polygons.

Below: Ushak carpet of the Lotto type; early 17th century. This type is recognizable by its particular decoration with characteristic yellow geometric arabesques against a red ground. The two

diagrams show the central part of the geometric arabesque (above) and the main border's cartouches (below), a motif used in Lotto carpets from the beginning of the 17th century.

however, the compositions began to lose their original severity, becoming more confused and disorderly. The oldest examples of small-pattern Holbeins are believed to have come from Ushak in west-central Anatolia, and Bergama (ancient capital of Pergamon), on the Aegean

coast, has been hypothesized as the provenance for the large-pattern Holbeins. Another group of carpets is referred to as Lotto carpets after the Venetian painter Lorenzo Lotto (ca. 1480-1556). These are of a single, easily recognizable form: standing out against a usually bright red field is a

yellow grid of geometric arabesques that take shape as rows of cruciform elements alternating with rows of octagonal or rhomboidal elements. The borders of the oldest examples (end of the 15th to the 16th century) have kufesque motifs, while the borders of those from the

ANATOLIA

Ushak medallion carpet; 16th-17th century. This type, made in court workshops, shows stylistic similarities to the Persian taste in the centralized arrangement and the markedly curvilinear and elaborate design. The round form of the medallion and the presence in the corners of halves of another four polylobate medallions, suggesting an endless repetition, are distinguishing traits.

beginning of the 17th century are decorated with the cartouche or cloudband motif. Lotto carpets were exported to the West in great numbers and were produced until the early 18th century. Also called arabesqued Ushaks, after the city of their provenance, these carpets bear witness to an art that had reached maturity and was capable of expressing new and more complex formulas while remaining true to the geometric spirit and decorative models of the Seljuk tradition.

Court production

In the 16th and 17th centuries the region of Ushak was the principal center of Anatolian production under the patronage of the sultan and Ottoman nobles. In refined court ateliers artist-designers worked out for master weavers new large-size decorations of a complex and refined character that was nearer, compared to the earlier carpets made in the local geometric style, to the floral style, the curvilinear designs then being developed in Persia.

Medallion Ushaks are the Anatolian carpets most similar to the contemporaneous Persian carpets. The field is bright red and thickly worked with minute blue floral designs

(in rare cases the two colours are inverted); at its center is a round medallion with a dark background, enlivened by yellow arabesques; near the corners of the field are the halves of another four secondary, multifoil medallions that suggest endless repetition. The curvilinear design, the floral elements, and most of all the central structure—all anomalous to the Anatolian language, which had been characterized by the repetition of one or more elementary modules since the earliest Seljuk carpets—have led to the theory that these carpets show the direct influence of Persian models from the Safavid court. According to recent studies, however

the medallion layouts seem to have been developed independently during the same period in Anatolia and Persia, perhaps on the basis of formulas that had arrived from central Asia in the 15th century. At any rate, this model was very successful and influenced later production; it was made, in increasingly coarse versions, from the middle of the 16th century to the end of the 18th.

Two other types similar to this were made during the same period: Ushaks with more than one medallion and star Ushaks. The first are characterized by the repetition along the central axis of the field of principal medallions that are round or, more often, ogival and have scalloped edges.

These are accompanied on the sides by two rows of secondary multifoil medallions, cut in half or in segments that correspond to the borders. Star Ushaks are also arranged in an elongated format; against a red background are balanced offset rows of eight-pointed starlike medallions with dark backgrounds that alternate with small cruciform elements. In this case, as in the preceding, the breaking of the medallions along the borders suggests endless repetition, thus making the design fit with the more traditional Anatolian language.

Two particular types

Within the vast range of the extremely lively and colourful Anatolian carpets are two particular types that are characterized by light backgrounds, white or ivory, on which are arranged small full-field designs framed by cloudband borders. These types are called the "bird"-pattern Ushak and the *chintamani* Ushak.

The first has vertical or horizontal rows of rosettes alternating with typical geometric leaves of an elongated form that were once erroneously believed to be stylized birds with folded wings and long

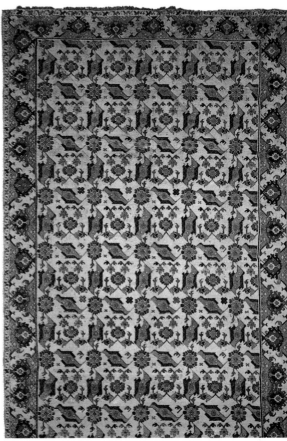

beaks. Known as the "bird" pattern, this type was widespread in the past, particularly during the 17th century.

The second type is distinguished by the

repetition of alternating rows of the *chinatami* motif. Antique examples are very rare today, but imitations that date to the beginning of the 20th century are numerous.

ANATOLIA

Ushak prayer rug; 17th century. The mihrab in Ushak prayer rugs is characterized by a keyhole shape in the lower portion, as shown in the diagram at bottom.

Opposite above: Ushak double-niche carpet; 17th century. The hexagonal medallion is typical, and the carpet assumes the form of a "classical" directional prayer rug when the sacred

lamp appears hanging from one end of the medallion (drawing).

Birth of the prayer rug

The first prayer rugs were made in Ushak during the 16th century. Also called Bellini rugs, after the Venetian painter Giovanni Bellini (ca. 1432-1516), they are decorated by a mihrab, usually red, within which is a medallion, and can be recognized by the form of the niche, the lower part of which resembles a keyhole and bears in turn a small medallion. The layout of the prayer rug also appears in the so-called Tintoretto rugs, named after another celebrated Venetian artist (1518-1594), which are more properly known as double-niche Ushaks because of the hexagonal shape of the medallion, a result of joining two specular niches. The use of a central rosette and four side ones creates the same type of nondirectional structure found in medallion carpets, but the mosque lamp hanging from the end of the rosette often gives these rugs the directional sense typical of prayer rugs. Usually small and decorated with cloudband borders, this 16th-century layout became widespread beginning in the 17th century.

Mameluke and floral carpets

Ushak was not the only center of carpet production

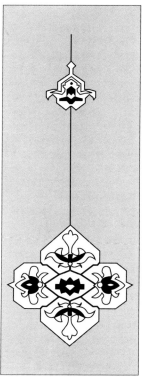

67

Below: Detail of a Mameluke carpet; Cairo, 16th century. The design, composed of many concentric or densely overlapping polygons, achieves a kaleidoscopic effect (diagram).

Bottom: Mameluke carpet; Cairo, 16th century. In this carpet the colours are restricted to red, yellow, and blue. The diagram shows the typical borders with geometric motifs.

for the court, and after the Ottoman conquest of Egypt (1517), the workshops of Cairo were added. These had already been operating at the time of the preceding Mameluke dynasty (1252-1517), under whom a very particular model had been created. The so-called Mameluke carpet, today extremely rare, is easy to recognize because its field is thickly occupied by various geometric figures (rhombuses, octagonals, squares, circles, etc) in differing sizes and united so as to create a typical kaleidoscopic effect. In the most common layout, the figures rotate around a central medallion formed in turn of many superimposed geometric figures. The colours used are lively but not numerous, often

Below: Fragment of a Mameluke carpet; Cairo, 15th-16th centuries. The kaleidoscopic effect of the Mameluke style is particularly clear; the diagram at left shows the close arrangement of many small octagons.
Bottom: Floral carpet; Cairo, 16th century. Typical of Persian influence is the adoption of the curvilinear style and naturalistic floral decorations. The diagram at right shows how the border was influenced by the herati motif born in Persia.

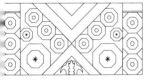

restricted to red, blue, and green only; the borders usually have the cartouche motif. These carpets, which are distinguished technically by the adoption of the asymmetrical knot, were made from the 15th century until the Ottoman conquest.

Because of their unique characteristics, Mameluke carpets are a case apart and cannot be included within the production of Anatolia. They present, instead, a meeting place of the geometric style shared by Anatolia and the asymmetrical technique typical of Persia.

Following the Ottoman conquest, the workshops of Cairo began producing carpets in a new style, one to which both the mature and refined taste of the new rulers and Persian decorative influences contributed. This carpet style, known as both the floral style and the Turkish court style, is characterized by naturalistic elements in curvilinear designs. Employing few colours and made using the asymmetrical knot like the earlier Mameluke carpets, the style adopted the Persian manner of ornament with flowers and leaves, arranged in repeating motifs or, more frequently, on medallion layouts or prayer rugs. Carpets were made in this style from the beginning of

A singular carpet

The layout and design of this interesting carpet indicate that it is one of the carpets made in Cairo in the floral style, also known as the Turkish court style. The small size of the central medallion with respect to the emphasis conferred on the rest of the field, the curvilinear decorations with floral arabesques, and the asymmetrical knotting leave no doubt. The carpet's singular crosslike shape, designed to cover the top of a table with four borders to drape over the sides, and the presence of four coats of arms (unfortunately unidentified), one on each arm at the center beneath the upper panel, indicate that it was made on commission and was destined for the home of a noble European family. During the Renaissance it was not rare for such "personalized" carpets to be commissioned by Westerners seeking prestige or by Orientals to use as gifts to wealthy Europeans, but such unusual shapes cannot have been common. Furthermore, the traditional history of this carpet is equally singular and is wrapped in legend. According to the account, Cesare Borgia received this carpet as a gift from Cardinal Orsini in 1502; Borgia, in turn, gave it to Niccolò Machiavelli, who brought it with him to San Gimignano when he moved to Florence (the carpet is today held in the civic museum of San Gimignano). This story has serious chronological problems, however, since stylistically the carpet is datable to the mid 16th century, while the events of the story claim it was made at least as early as 1502. Even so, the carpet bears witness to the high level of refinement achieved by the court workshops of Cairo under the Ottoman domination.

*Melas prayer rug;
19th century. From
the 17th century
onward the design of
prayer rugs began to
grow complicated, as
indicated by this
example from Melas,
in which the mihrab is*

*broken into three
separate cusps, as
shown in the diagram
at bottom.*

the 16th century until the
end of the 17th.

"Minor" production

During the 17th century,
together with the
outstanding carpets made
at court in specialized
workshops under
commissions from the
Ottoman nobility, another
kind of carpet production
began to appear. This
production is often
somewhat improperly
referred to as "minor," for it
was more ordinary; however,
the carpets were always of
excellent quality and were
made both for domestic use
and export. These carpets
were made in the various
levels of workshops located
in cities and villages
throughout the region of
Anatolia. Of small or
medium size, they were
characterized by fidelity to
the traditional geometric
style, which translated into
stylized forms both the
designs created in the great
workshops and the
naturalistic motifs of
Persian influence.

The major representatives
of this production are
Transylvanian carpets and
prayer rugs. Transylvanian
(or Siebenbürgen) carpets
are named for the region of
Transylvlania, which was
then an Ottoman province
and where they were found
in abundance; they seem to
have been made, however,
in the Anatolian city of

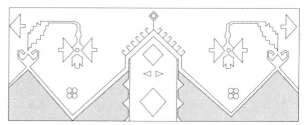

Bergama, from which they
were exported. These small-
size carpets rarely have a
single-niche layout and far
more frequently have an
unusual double-niche
structure. It has therefore
become common use to

apply the name
Transylvanian to a particular
type of double-niche carpet.
This type is a descendent of
antique Ushaks but displays
greater geometric sensitivity
and less attention to
calligraphy, aspects that

71

Prayer rug with coupled columns; Ladik (?), end 17th century. The elaborate prayer rugs of this type are characterized by an architectural mihrab divided into several arches by means of long, thin coupled columns, as shown in the diagram.

together confer a certain rigidity to the whole design, the outstanding element of which is a large central hexagonal medallion containing stylized geometric or floral elements. The most common colours are red, yellow, and ivory; the main border is usually decorated with a cartouche motif, including geometric figures similar to crabs or more or less stylized floral designs. Such Transylvanian carpets were made between the first half of the 17th century and the beginning of the 18th, but the model derived, known as a double-niche Transylvanian, was greatly imitated in later centuries.

Prayer rugs had already appeared in Ushak, but it was in the minor production centers of Anatolia beginning in the 17th century that the form underwent greatly increased production, with forms that varied from place to place. In a short time this model became the most significant and most widely adopted in Anatolia, representing a union of that region's religious spirit and geometric tradition, although the new floral style imported from Persian also played a part. Thus the niche on these carpets can be variously formed using columns, corbels, and differing shapes of arches

(acute, stepped, pointed like arrowheads, like an inverted V, and so on), and the field can host, aside from the traditional sacred mosque lamp and variously decorated water basins, more or less complex and stylized floral elements. The niches can be simple or complicated with coupled columns, and there can be one niche or, as is the case with saph carpets, several. In carpets with coupled columns the mihrab is presented in a more elaborate and more architectural design, with a portal subdivided by very thin double columns that bear in turn, usually, three arches in the form of cusps.

*Detail of Ushak saph,
or multiple prayer
rug; 17th century.
Saphs are easily
recognized because of
their decoration,
composed of the
alignment of several
mihrabs, which can be
elaborately decorated
or shaped, or very
simple, as in this
example, in which the
niches are defined
only by the sharp
chromatic contrast.*

The origin of this layout is obscure, but it is known to have been widespread in Anatolia beginning in the middle of the 17th century, and it enjoyed great commercial success, proven by the fact that the oldest examples were found in Transylvania.

In saph carpets, the niche, regardless of its style, is repeated several times, its form unchanging, all across the surface of the carpet, thus forming a continuous series of niches side by side: saph is Turkish for "row" or "in a row." Also known as multiple prayer rugs or family prayer rugs, because they were initially believed to have been made for the group performance of Muslim rites, saph carpets were a popular style from the 17th century to the end of the 18th, after which they declined.

With simple layouts or coupled columns, the many antique and old prayer rugs have been grouped based on their stylistic differences (form of the niche, of the arch, border design, internal decorations), and classified according to the centers of provenance. The oldest specimens come from Ghiordes, Kula, and Ladik.

Old carpets

No new styles were introduced during the 1700s, but toward the end of the century the so-called

ANATOLIA

Below: Ghiordes prayer rug; end 19th century. The transformation of the mihrab, the realistic flowers, and the pastel tints are characteristics of the Majid style.

Opposite: Ghiordes double-niche carpet; end 18th century. The naturalistic flowers show French influence. The vine border is typical of Ghiordes carpets from the 18th to the 19th century.

Turkish baroque began to take hold, reflecting the enormous influence of French art. Several decorative elements taken from that distant world were adapted for use in carpets, and traditional motifs were reinterpreted "in the French style." The 1800s, marked by the progressive decline of the Ottoman Empire and by the decadence of the workshops of Ushak, saw the definitive affirmation of French influence in the birth of the Majid style, named for the Ottoman sultan Abd al-Majid I (reigned 1839-1861). A dedicated lover of French art in its more ostentatious and refined aspects, he imposed it as the model for all artistic forms. Around the middle of the century a hybrid style came into use that involved the insertion of naturalistic floral elements and the introduction of pastel tints in a close adherence to the style of Savonnerie and Aubusson carpets. Made in city workshops (such as Ghiordes, Kirshehir, and Melas), carpets in this Majid style are characterized by layouts so stylized and transformed that they are almost unrecognizable (most frequent in prayer rugs) and by decorations using realistic leaves and flowers of Western taste. The small centers of carpet

production, however, were unaffected by all these innovations, and their carpets remained faithful to the traditional geometric style, as did the carpets made by nomads, the oldest examples of which date to the 19th century. On the contrary, the imperial workshops of

Hereke, set up around the middle of the 19th century, went so far as to make copies of Aubusson, Savonnerie, and Persian carpets. From the beginning of the 1900s to the fall of the Ottoman Empire in 1922, the carpet production of Anatolia began to register a growing

Bergama double-niche carpets; end 19th century. Typical of these carpets are the obvious predilection for muted colours and the use of Caucasian border motifs, such as

the serrated leaf (diagram).

general adaptation to the requests and tastes of the Western market, which involved increasing imitation of Persian models from the classical period. This phenomenon did not take place among the nomads, who remained tenaciously anchored to geometric forms and traditional designs, because they were still uninvolved in the great commerce and exportation toward the West.

Major production areas

Based on stylistic similarities, the carpets made in Anatolia can be divided into three geographic production areas: western, central, and eastern Anatolia. The traditional types made in the most important centers within each area are examined in the following sections.

Western Anatolia

Area of Bergama. The area of ancient Pergamon is distinguished by its fidelity to the layouts and decorative motifs of the classical era: small- and large-pattern Holbeins, carpets with double niches, and prayer rugs with the typical keyhole design. The borders are decorated by stars and rosettes along with motifs imported from the Caucasus, such as

Kiz carpets

Kiz carpets get their name from the Turkish word kiz, which means "girl" or, more precisely, "girl of marriageable age." The name is used conventionally for wedding carpets, part of a bride's dowry. It was common custom on the wedding day for the bride to give her groom one or more carpets, according to her financial means, that she had made herself. These carpets are thus not products of court ateliers or great workshops, but are "village" carpets, made in homes in small centers, destined for private family use, and without any commercial or commemorative intent. Datable to the beginning of the 19th century and usually characterized by a double-niche layout inherited from antique Transylvanian carpets, these special carpets were made in a great variety of designs based on the traditions of various production areas. The Kiz-Ghiordes, for example, such as the carpet shown here, which

is datable to the beginning of the 19th century, are characterized by a pale ground (usually white), a central hexagon or double niche (diagram), and typical decoration using tiny black designs called **sinekli**, which means "fleas" in Turkish; the same motif decorates the special pale or white strips that run zigzag across the width of the main border. Natural cotton was often used to achieve the characteristic white grounds, as it is more luminous than wool. Further distinctive elements are the carnations and stylized **boteh**, located in the four triangular areas at the sides of the central hexagon.

ANATOLIA

Ghiordes prayer rugs; 19th century. These are easily recognizable because of the squat and squarish shape of the niche and the use of numerous borders decorated with stylized floral elements or with the typical cubukli motif (as in the example at left).

serrated leaves and leaves alternating with winecups.

Ghiordes. Because of their elegance, carpets from Ghiordes were among the first to find favour in the West, so much so that the name Ghiordes is still used today, although inaccurately, for the type of symmetrical knot used in Anatolia. Ghiordes prayer rugs can be recognized by the importance given the numerous borders and for the resulting reduced size of the niche. The niche, highly geometric, is characterized by a reversed-V arch resting on squared shoulders, while a row of small flowers

(usually carnations) is arranged along the internal edge, and the sacred lamp is often transformed into a bunch of flowers. Above and below the niche are rectangular panels decorated by the cloudband motif or, later, by stylized floral elements. Until early in the 19th century the borders were often decorated by *cubukli* motifs; these were later replaced by stylized floral decorations, rendered increasingly realistic over the course of the 19th century following the Majid style. Ghiordes prayer rugs were among those most imitated from the 19th century onward by

other production areas, especially that of Panderma.

Area of Melas. This area is characterized by the predominance of warm colours, running from gold yellow to brick red. Melas prayer rugs can be recognized by their arrowhead-shaped niche, formed by the sudden narrowing of the arch. The niche is usually rust colour and topped by a pale area decorated with stylized floral elements. The main border has a rosette motif or large geometric flowers.

Hereke. This relatively recent production area (it dates

78

Melas prayer rug; end 19th-early 20th century. These carpets are recognizable by the arrowhead shape of the niche and the use of rather warm colours. The main border usually has rosettes or large geometric flowers (as in the diagram at bottom).

A comparison of two niches

The mihrab (or niche) is a fundamental element of prayer rugs. The shapes and sizes of the niches in Anatolian carpets vary according to the production center. For example, those of Melas are narrow, and the arch forms an "arrowhead" (above); in Ghiordes they are squat and squarish (below).

Hereke medallion carpet; 19th century. Hereke carpets can easily be distinguished from other Anatolian carpets because they use the asymmetrical knot and have refined decoration taken from the French or, more often, Persian tradition, as in this example, in which cloudbands, palmettes, and other floral elements predominate in a pure curvilinear style.

from the period between the mid-19th century and beginning of the 20th) is distinguished by the elegance of its carpets, which were made using the asymmetrical knot and sometimes employ silk and gold. The style was inspired by foreign floral taste, both Persian and French; many examples are copies of Kerman, Tabriz, Savonnerie, and Aubusson carpets.

Panderma prayer rug; end 19th-early 20th century. Imitations of Ghiordes prayer rugs, they are distinguished by their thin, ribbonlike columns and realistic sacred lamp.

stylized flowers alternating with three carnations. The most common layouts in antique examples are double niche, while hexagonal medallions or superimposed medallions appear in later examples. The central medallion is usually red and rests on a blue or dark brown background.

Area of Ushak. This area created a great many of the ancient types that became classic. Later examples are only tired and sterile repetitions of those models.

Kula. Kula prayer rugs are distinguished by long, narrow geometric niches. The niche rests on a field spread with small stylized flowers, and within the niche itself are other flowers, gathered at the center to form the tree of life, which is often flanked by two ribbonlike floral columns. The borders are decorated with carnations or other stylized floral elements; the most typical element is a kind of border decoration, often located in a minor border, which consists of a motif inexplicably called an alligator motif, which is composed of a narrow multicolour arabesque formed by the unwinding of highly stylized palmettes, joined one to the other in three or four different colours. Examples with

Panderma. This area cannot boast of an antique tradition, having begun production in the 19th century, but it merits note for its prayer rugs made in imitation of antique examples. Similar to the Ghiordes in the square shape of the niche, Pandermas have a reversed-T or ogival arch and within the niche are often two small ribbonlike side columns; the sacred lamp hangs realistically at the center of the vault. The main border is usually decorated with stylized floral elements. The colours are somewhat pale and without contrasts, an effect often achieved using procedures of artificial bleaching to create a more "antique" appearance.

Demirci. Carpets from this area can be recognized by the decorative motif of the main border: on a yellow or blue background is drawn a red zigzagging tendril from which grow groups of three

Below: Kula prayer
rug; 18th century.
These can be
recognized by the
narrow, elongated
shape of the mihrab,
which contains a
stylized tree of life
and is subdivided by

characteristic
ribbonlike columns.
Also typical is the
"alligators" decoration
of the minor border.

Bottom: Kula double-
niche carpet; 18th
century. Also in this
layout the form of the
mihrab is narrow and
elongated.

subtle *cubukli* frames appeared around the middle of the 19th century. Aside from several 18th-century examples, most Kula carpets date to the 19th century. Also made during those centuries were double-niche Kulas, characterized by a long, narrow central medallion most often set against a red or blue background.

Area of Megri. Carpets from this 19th-century area of production, also known as "Rhodes" carpets, are unusual. The prayer rugs are distinguished by their narrow, long niches often in flanking pairs inside which are various decorative motifs from geometric flowers and trees to octagonal medallions with rosettes. The outermost border has a white background and often bears a local motif shaped

Ladik prayer rug; end 19th century. The fundamental element in these carpets is the use of stylized tulips, which appear alternating with cusps in the panel under the niche (diagram at left) and often also in the borders. The main border is usually decorated with stylized floral motifs, as shown in the diagram at bottom.

like a kind of fret with triangular elements.

Central Anatolia

Ladik. The ornamental element characteristic of this production area is the stylized tulip, which appears in the field and borders. In prayer rugs these flowers appear standing on long straight stems alternating with cusps in rectangular panels above or below the niche. Ladik prayer rugs usually appear in one of two variants determined by the design of the mihrab: in the first, simpler variant, the arch is stepped and the background is solid or contains a stylized floral element; in the second, derived from antique prayer rugs with coupled columns, the niche is made of three geometric arches, the

The flowers of the Ottomans

Carnations and tulips are the flowers that get the lion's share in the fields and borders of Anatolian carpets, exceeding in frequency of use pomegranates, roses, and imaginary flowers. Carnations, almost always red and shown open or closed, in frontal or profile views, can be recognized by the irregular shape of the corollas, which are often notched or serrated. They appear most frequently in the carpets from Ghiordes, Kirshehir, and Demirci, usually arranged in bouquets, rows, or isolated positions; small identical carnations are sometimes arranged along the internal edge of the mihrab on Ghiordes prayer rugs. Tulips (often mistaken for lilies in Western interpretations) characterize primarily the carpets made in Ladik and can have typical multicoloured calyxes, more or less stylized, that stand upright on long stems, as in the spaces located under the niches in Ladik prayer rugs, or they can be grouped in bouquets or arranged along tendrils in the border decorations of carpets from various production areas. Aside from any symbolic meaning, carnations and tulips were used as simple decorative motifs in general in Ottoman art, but of all the traditional ornamental flowers, they were the subjects most loved both by the artists and the people who

commissioned their works. Carnations and tulips were thus used not only in carpets, but also in the linen and velvet textiles produced in Anatolia between the 17th and

19th century, as well as in the multicolour ceramic tiles that became a characteristic element of Ottoman style and art.

Konya carpet with three medallions; 19th century. Faithful to the oldest geometric tradition, Konya carpets can be recognized by their polygonal decorative motifs, often hooked and usually incorporating an eight-pointed star, as shown in the two diagrams below.

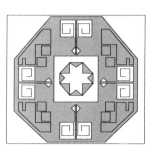

central of which is wider. The colours are brilliant and contrasting, based on red, yellow, and blue.

Area of Konya. Until the 19th century and even later this area of antique production succeeded in maintaining its own tradition, which can be traced to the pure geometric style of Seljuk derivation. These carpets are decorated with large elementary polygons, often stepped and hooked, arranged in pairs or rows. Konya carpets are often distinguished by their borders, decorated by a typical "shield" motif formed of a series of pentagonal or trianglar geometric motifs arranged in rows.

Kirshehir. The shape of the mihrab in the prayer rugs from this area, a stepped arch outlined in white and topped by an arrowhead, is very similar to that of the prayer rugs of Mudjur, as is the rectangular panel decorated with other arrowheads. Many other elements, however, are unique to Kirshehir prayer rugs, such as the presence in the field of stylized carnations, which also appear in bunches of three in the typical yellow-background border, often accompanied by a *cubukli* frames of different colours. The palette is not particularly vivid, except in the Majid-style examples,

ANATOLIA

which also make greater use of floral elements.

Mudjur. Typical of this area are prayer rugs, which were produced from the beginning of the 19th century. The upper part of the niches is outlined in white and has a stepped arch that ends in a small, characteristic arrowhead; the same motif is repeated in a narrow panel above the niche. The borders are very striking and colourful, in particular the main border, which is often decorated with a motif of large rosettes inscribed within rectangles or squares.

Eastern Anatolia

The stylistic situation in this area is decidedly complex, since it is influenced from the north by the Caucasus and from the south by Persia and is inhabited primarily by nomadic or seminomadic populations of various origins. For this reason, centers, areas, or tribes to which carpets can be attributed cannot be established with certainty. The carpets from this area do have in common a very elementary geometric decoration worked out with combinations of two to five rows of polygonal medallions using subdued or only slightly contrasting colours, including a type of type of aubergine violet.

Prayer rugs are rare, and they are small and somewhat elongated. By convention, the rougher-made carpets are attributed to the Yuruk nomadic population.

Kars. Kars represents the single exception to the stylistic confusion in eastern

Below: Yuruk double-niche carpet; end 19th-beginning 20th century. Typical elements of these nomad-made carpets are the simple decoration, with concentric polygonal medallions and motifs imported from the Caucasus (such as the serrated leaves along the border), and the muted range of colours, almost always including violet.

Bottom: Kars medallion carpet; beginning 19th century. Similar to Kazaks from the Caucasus for the limiting of the elements to large polygonal forms, Kars can be distinguished by their light grounds and muted colours.

Anatolia. This ancient production center, which together with the Caucasus created the dragon carpets in the 16th to 17th centuries, distinguished itself by the creation in 19th century of the so-called Turkish Kazaks, which were similar to the carpets of the same name from the Caucasus but differed from them by their pale backgrounds and the use of somewhat dull colours.

ANATOLIA

Antique carpets

Later carpets

USHAK

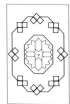

Small-pattern Holbein carpet; 16th century. Typical: Kufic borders and heart-shaped medallion.

Lotto-type carpet with arabesques; 16th-17th century. Typical: border with cartouches and arabesques

GHIORDES

Prayer rug; 19th century. Typical: *cubukli* borders and squat and squarish niche.

Majid-style prayer rug; end 19th century. Typical: floral border and internal vase of flowers.

Prayer rug; 17th century. Typical: border and keyhole lower area of the niche.

"Bird" carpet; 16th-17th century. Typical: border and decorative motif repeated in the field.

BERGAMA

MELAS

Double-niche carpet; 19th century. Typical: border and antique Anatolian geometric motifs.

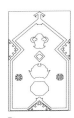

Prayer rug; end 19th-early 20th century. Typical: border with geometric flowers and arrowhead niche.

ANATOLIA

Antique carpets

Later carpets

HEREKE

Medallion carpet; 19th century. Typical: border and decorative motifs in curvilinear style.

KULA

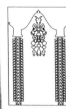

Prayer rug; 18th century. Typical: "alligators" border and niche with ribbonlike columns.

YURUK

Double-niche carpet; end 19th-early 20th century. Typical: border with serrated leaves and geometric medallion.

KARS

Medallion carpet; early 20th century. Typical: border and geometric medallions.

LADIK

Prayer rug; end 19th century. Typical: floral border and presence of tulips.

KONYA

Three-medallion carpet; 19th century. Typical: border and geometric medallion.

KIRSHEHIR

 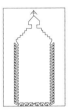

Prayer rug; 19th century. Typical: the border with bouquets of carnations and the white-outlined niche.

MUDJUR

Prayer rug; end 18th century. Typical: the border with rosettes and the panel with arrowheads.

PERSIA

♦ Based on a somewhat superficial and biased judgment, Persian carpets are commonly held to be "the carpet" *par excellence*. In reality, they share their central role in the stylistic and historical development of the knotted carpet with their Anatolian rivals and counterparts.

The expression of an art and a social tradition more than of a religious belief, Persian carpets are distinguished by their extremely complex and calligraphic nature, with the main emphasis on design and line. Persian weavers have sometimes exploited the geometric style in the form of abstract or stylized figures in the field, but it is the curvilinear style that has proved the most successful, since it offers the most suitable means of

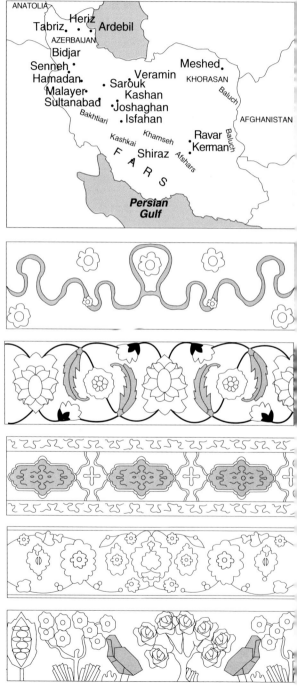

Diagram of the asymmetrical, or Senneh, knot, the one most used in Persia.

Right: From top to bottom. Five borders: cloudband, herati, cartouche, palmette, figural.

interpreting the particularly poetic and naturalistic spirit of the region.

The result has been the development of a great number of very elaborate decorations, the most common being thin, highly intricate arabesques, on which medallions of various shapes, palmettes, and other abstract decorative motifs are arranged; but Persian carpets also include realistically portrayed flowers and animals, since the Shiite branch of Islam, which is the dominant sect in Persia, unlike the Sunnites in Anatolia, allows for greater freedom of expression and even tolerates the representation of the human figure, which from the 19th century onward even occupied a primary position in terms of size and importance to the rest of the decoration.

The wide variety of colours, large numbers of which are used in each carpet, are never garish and never clash; rather than being used across broad areas, they are arranged with imagination and careful balance in small contiguous areas, usually outlined in black. Red and blue are, in general, the major colours and are arranged so as to make pale patterns stand out against dark fields. There is less elaboration of colour in nomadic carpets, in which abstract geometric or stylized designs clearly predominate. The most widely used knot is the asymmetrical; in many areas (particularly in the west and northwest), however, the symmetrical knot is used. The materials used are wool, cotton, and silk with the addition of gold and silver thread in certain early examples. The carpets vary widely in size: the early court examples are of markedly larger dimensions, while the nomadic works are smaller. The medallion layout is the most common, with interpretations that are more or less geometric or curvilinear, in both abstract and naturalistic styles, according to the area of production.

The style of a great dynasty

Despite the absence of any examples definitely attributable to the 16th century, we know from

93

PERSIA

Below: Palmette carpet; eastern Persia (Herat?), end 16th-early 17th century. At the beginning of the 16th century, with the birth of the Safavid style, the decorative structure of Persian

carpets began to be based on intertwining stalks and flowering branches, and these ultimately came to completely fill the field and borders.

Bottom: Kerman medallion carpet; 19th century. The arabesques, floral decoration, realistic animals, and harmonious colours are typical of the Persian style.

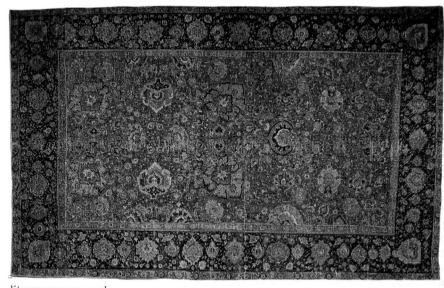

literary sources, and especially from 14th- and 15th-century miniatures, that in very early times Persia must have possessed weavers capable of creating geometric carpets very similar to those made in Anatolia during the Seljuk era. The first signs of a new stylistic language may have begun to appear at the end of the 15th century, but it was following the rise of the magnificent and long-lasting Safavid dynasty (1502-1722), which united the nation, that the Persian carpet really achieved its independence, exploiting the decorative inspiration previously provided by the other Persian arts (most notably books and ceramics) as well as the decorative influences arriving from China, such as cloudbands, peonies, lotus flowers, and other elements

of a naturalistic character. In this way the carpet became one of the most important expressions of Safavid art and society, achieving the zenith of its development during the brilliant reign of Shah Abbas the Great (1587-1629). Inspired by the subtle arabesque motifs and floral patterns used to decorate the borders of miniatures and the embossed-leather covers of books, the art of carpet making, which became a particular focus of attention, was obliged to revise completely its traditional severe geometrical structures in order to adapt to the new curvilinear tendencies. The new decorative structure was superimposed on networks of slender stems and flowering branches, whose endless, symmetrical intertwinings covered the entire field, which gradually filled up with flowers of every sort and with palmettes, animals, and tiny human figures. The new calligraphic influence brought out the creation of a decoration based on densely interwoven lines and patterns rather than on the juxtaposition of colours. Borders began to assume particular importance, displaying a wide variety of decorative motifs that were invariably chosen in order to show off the highly complex arabesques of the

The islimi motif

The arabesques that have so much importance in Persian carpets can also take on special shapes, as is the case with the islimi motif. It consists simply of a stem twisted around itself in a spiral, usually ending in two forked leaves that often continue and complicate the overall design. Whether extremely thin and calligraphic or thick and more overt, islimi motifs in general are accompanied by flowers and leaves; in carpet decoration they usually appear multiplied in complex arabesques in the field (especially around the central medallion); less often they are found repeated in smaller sizes in the main border. The motif is also known as aslimi or eslimi, but the name's precise meaning remains obscure. Some scholars think it comes from the word Islam, since it is a motif typical of Islamic arts in general, but this is a hypothesis born in the West. Others claim it is in some way related to a sultan named Selim or a miniaturist named Aslim; still others give it the meaning of "serpentine," since its form resembles that of a twisted snake, or "branch" or "bud," because it is used as a plant element. Whatever its derivation, it appeared in Persian carpets during the 16th century, if not earlier, first in somewhat rigid forms, but it was used chiefly in the 17th century with a decidedly curvilinear and complex design. It was brought back into use during the 19th century, finding application in the carpets made in Kerman and Meshed; even today it is one of the antique Persian designs most often imitated.

*Below: Detail of a
medallion carpet;
northwestern Persia
(Tabriz?), 16th
century. From the
16th century onward,
the Persian
calligraphic
sensibility found*

*expression in the
curvilinear style, here
magnificently
represented.*

*Bottom: Detail of
cartouche carpet;
northwestern Persia
(Tabriz?), early 16th
century. The Safavid
style is distinguished
by complexity,
refinement, and an
elegant effect.*

interior to their best advantage. This curvilinear or floral style also permitted the creation of more realistic designs capable of satisfying the naturalistic taste of the Persians.

These decorative innovations also brought about a major technical revolution that revealed itself in three main aspects. First was the adoption of silk for both the foundation and pile of the most prized examples, which had the effect of allowing for finer knotting and thus a far more detailed and minute type of decoration. Second was the establishment of court workshops in the most important cities, such as Tabriz, Isfahan, Kashan, Kerman, and Herat, where highly trained craftsmen were employed to create finely knotted carpets for the Safavid nobility. Third was the division of the carpet-making process into two separate phases: the design and the actual weaving. Court miniaturists were commissioned to create the designs which, after conversion into cartoons, were used as models for weavers employed in the imperial workshops. This distinction between the role of the creative artist and the working craftsman had never been applied to the production of carpets, which until then had always been tied to patterns passed

The Ardebil carpet

The magnificent Ardebil carpet is one of the great masterpieces of the art of knotting from both the technical and decorative points of view. Very large (34 feet 6 inches x 17 feet 6 inches), it has a silk foundation and wool pile; the knotting system is of the asymmetrical type. A cartouche located near the end of one of the short sides of the field bears, together with several poetic verses, the date 946 (which corresponds to 1539-1540 of the Christian era) and a name: "Maksud of Kashan," perhaps the creator of the design or the buyer of the carpet. According to some scholars, the carpet was donated by "Maksud" to the mosque in the Persian city of Ardebil, from which the carpet takes its name, but this is no more than a hypothesis. Also in discussion is its provenance, debated between Tabriz and Kashan. The sumptuous decoration of the carpet

represents the stylistic zenith reached by a Persian medallion layout. The central rosette, divided into 16 sections, is surrounded by 16 almond-shaped pendants. Along the longitudinal axis are two mosque lamps, and from the

corners of the field spread quarter sections of the central medallion; the rest of the field is enlivened by an intricate arabesque decorated by small floral elements. Three minor borders, one decorated with the cloudband motif, accompany the main border, decorated with cartouches of various shape. The colours are very varied and harmonized; standing out against the intense blue of the ground is the yellow of the medallion and the corner sections and the different colours of the other designs, with a decided predominance of red and blue. The general effect is at once imposing and harmonious. The carpet came to England at the end of the last century and is now in the Victoria and Albert Museum of London; a twin carpet, unfortunately very fragmentary, is in the Los Angeles County Museum of Art.

n through memorization r generations or created ontaneously on the loom, nd it represented the reatest point of divergence etween town and court arpets and those produced villages or by nomads. Constantly searching for ew decorative effects and otected by Safavid atronage, the great Persian tists devised highly omplex designs and

introduced wide ranges of colour, often transforming their carpets into pages on which to write religious and poetic verses. In addition, these masters sometimes signed and dated their creations, thus further establishing them as true works of art. This important step, first taken in Persia during the 16th century, had a radical effect on the very meaning of carpets, which

went from being an item linked traditionally to worship and daily life to being a social emblem of the wealthy, a luxury object, often made using gold and silver thread, destined to adorn the palaces and open-air pavilions of the Persian court or to act as magnificent presentation gifts with which to dazzle the rulers of the great nations of Europe. The close

PERSIA

connection between the nobility of the day and the art of the carpet is further confirmed by history: when Safavid patronage began to wane around the middle of the 17th century, the great era of carpet-making began to show its first signs of decline, and carpet production went into a crisis after 1722, at the time of the Afghan invasion and the eclipse of the dynasty whose greatest symbol had been precisely those carpets.

Antique types

Today, any discussion of the earliest Persian carpets must speak in terms of rarity, partly because of the intentionally precious nature of those carpets. It is no coincidence, for example, that all the surviving examples from the Safavid era are now held in great collections. They cannot be classified according to production center with any certainty because identical models were employed and circulated among many workshops; because similar working techniques were used; and because the characteristics of the finished carpets were so often the same, including their large sizes and the use of silk and precious-metal threads. The leading workshops during the Safavid period were at Tabriz, Kashan, Kerman,

Herat, Isfahan, and Joshaghan, but the differences among the carpets made in these places are superficial. The carpets of Tabriz are marked by an unusual chromatic severity and a certain rigidity of design; those from Kashan are characterized by a more imaginative and open style and are made almost exclusively of silk with elegance and

sumptuousness. It is difficult to distinguish between carpets from Herat and Isfahan because both use the same floral elements, although the former may display a more lively sense of composition and the latter a certain excessiveness, almost a baroque fullness. Joshaghan is known for using certain designs, but these were occasionally copied by other centers. The best,

Medallion carpet;
central Persia
(Kashan?), mid-16th
century. The Persian
interpretation of the
medallion layout is
rigorously centralized
(as shown in the
diagram),

curvilinear, and often
accompanied by
floral decoration and
highly realistic
animals.

albeit incomplete, form of classification, therefore, must be based on decorative types, subdividing the examples into medallion, animal and hunting, garden and tree-and-shrub, vase, floral, Polish, and Portuguese carpets. While these types were later imitated in every area and in every period, they never afterward achieved the technical perfection and inventive energy of that far-off golden age.

Medallion carpets

These large, elongated carpets (average length 157-95 inches) are characterized by a field thickly spread with flowers and arabesques and often peopled by animals and human figures; the field is dominated by a central medallion that can appear in

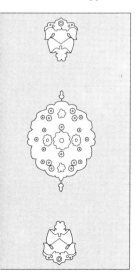

a variety of different shapes—star or circular, multifoil, or ogival—but which always stands out against the rest of the composition because of its size and the way in which its colour contrasts with the background. In most cases the medallion ends in two pendants, positioned longitudinally so as to provide the carpet with an axis of symmetry, and is accompanied by fractions of four other medallions, of either similar or different shape, placed at the corners in order to confer a particular sense of indefiniteness to the composition. The borders, fairly broad in size, usually display floral elements or cartouches and often contain inscriptions.

This type, which also evolved independently in Anatolia during the same period, was influenced in Persia by the decorative motifs of miniatures and, in particular, by the patterns on book covers, which meant that it differed from its Anatolian counterpart by its greater feeling of balance and its more highly developed sense of centrality and completeness. First introduced during the early years of the 16th century, a period that coincided with the rise of the Safavids, its main centers of production were Tabriz, Kashan, Kerman, and Herat. Because of its success, this design

became a Persian classic and a preferred prototype in every century.

Animal and hunting carpets

Thanks to the greater freedom of expression introduced by their Safavid patrons and by the Shiite religion, the Persian artists of the 16th century created two other, very similar designs, both of which

proved successful. Animal carpets, which have no central medallion and are arranged according to a directional layout, are characterized by a full-field decoration of arabesques or, more often, naturalistic bushes and other plant elements in the midst of which move creatures of every sort: wild animals, sometimes fighting one another, fabled and mythical beasts, even domestic animals. These figures, their colours contrasting with those of the ground, originally had more than a purely decorative significance, being symbolic allusions to a superior world and order. The specialist workshops in which these carpets were produced were mainly at Tabriz, where animals played a more important role than the floral elements; Herat, where floral elements were given more importance than the animals; and Kashan and Isfahan.

Hunting carpets or, more correctly, carpets with hunting scenes, are in reality a particular type of medallion carpet in which, apart from the usual dense mass of arabesques or naturalistic floral elements, the design of the field takes the form of curious vignettes of horsemen armed with lances and bows, portrayed either hunting down their prey or battling wild beasts. In creating these carpets, artists drew inspiration not only from contemporary miniatures and literature, but also from the

PERSIA

sumptuous life at court, albeit within the context of a symbolic reference to Eden and paradise. The weavers of Kashan were the leading specialists in this type of carpet.

Garden carpets and tree-and-shrub carpets

These two carpet types are closely related in terms of both their subject matter and their symbolism, for both of them allude to paradise and take their inspiration—having been made in a largely semidesert region—from the luxuriant parks that surrounded the palaces of the shahs.

In garden carpets the field is divided up into four, six, or more sections by streams, ponds, and fountains, with each compartment containing different species of realistically portrayed flowers and plants, and the streams, ponds, and fountains are in turn populated by naturalistically depicted fish and waterfowl. The surviving examples probably were made at Kerman and are datable to the 17th century, with the shapes becoming increasingly stylized during the course of the 18th century.

The same centuries also saw the development of a much more geometrical interpretation of this style employing less lively colours, which is attributable to the Kurdistan region and is characterized by large numbers of schematic compartments containing small, polygonal medallions and highly stylized plant elements.

Tree-and-shrub carpets, which also developed during the 16th century, are to all intents and purposes a refinement of the garden carpet, but without the animal elements. Various trees, most often cypresses and willows, interspersed with flowering shrubs, are arranged in directional patterns or around a central medallion; in 17th-century examples, however, the dominant composition was one of horizontal rows, symmetrically arranged. The origin of this type probably lies in eastern Persia, but its more geometrical variant, in which the plants alternate with rows of small medallions, is attributed to Kurdistan and dated to between the end of the 16th and beginning of the 17th centuries.

Vase carpets

A distinction must first be made between carpets made using the vase technique and carpets made using the vase design.

102

Tree-and-shrub carpet; northeastern Persia (Herat?), early 16th century. This type is characterized by the presence of realistic trees arranged in symmetrical rows.

Cypresses and willows are the most popular.

103

PERSIA

The former are distinguished only by the special way in which they are worked: they are characterized by three passes of weft for every row of knots, with the outer knots tightened and the central one left slack. The warp, being on two levels, creates a characteristic ribbing on the reverse. This technique is not associated with any particular decorative pattern, and the surviving examples are decorated with different motifs, including medallions, gardens, floral elements, and so on; but because the earliest examples bear a vase design, the word *vase* has come to be applied quite erroneously to the technique used in their manufacture. Characterized by an extremely bright and varied range of colours, these carpets have been very tentatively ascribed to Kerman; their dating, also the subject of considerable controversy, ranges from the end of the 16th to the beginning of the 18th century.

Carpets made using the vase design, on the other hand, form a definite decorative category and are not necessarily made using the technique described above. They are characterized by an ascending directional layout: from the bottom, along one of the short sides, pairs of

very long stems, often emerging from elegant vases, develop toward the opposite side. Intersecting at regular intervals, these stems create a sort of regular latticework, more or less curvilinear and extended across the entire field, that modulates and organizes the thick distribution of leaves,

palmettes, and naturalistic floral elements. Probably first developed at the end of the 16th century during the reign of Shah Abbas the Great, this design has been variously attributed to Joshaghan and Kerman. Its production continued until the beginning of the 18th century and had great

The Shah Abbas palmette

During the reign of Shah Abbas I the Great (1587-1629), the Persian court's greatest miniature artists amused themselves by creating luxurious and elaborate designs to transfer to carpets; aside from devoting themselves to new decorative inventions, they turned in some cases to the transformation and stylistic adaptation of motifs that were already known and consolidated by the general artistic tradition. Among these was the palmette, an ancient floral motif inspired by the fan-shaped leaves of the palm or the lily. When the palmette first appeared in carpets at the beginning of the 16th century its form was still somewhat rigid, but by the end of that century it had become lusher, so much so that it was transformed into the leading floral element in carpet decoration. The artists of the court of Shah Abbas elaborated the palmette into richer and

more naturalistic forms, creating palmettes still slightly closed, as though budding, and therefore of elongated form, and "flaming" palmettes, by which was meant those already flowering, with open corollas fringed with numerous petals spread in a sunburst. These new floral elements, designed in honor of the sovereign, were baptized Shah Abbas palmettes. In the decoration of carpets they are used joined by curvilinear vines and ornamented with falciform leaves. The new composition enjoyed great success in all Persian carpets, even during later centuries, and its basic design came to be called the Shah Abbas design.

influence on the stylistic trends of later centuries.

Floral carpets

The numerous examples of this style, among the best known and liked of Persian carpets, are characterized by full-field decoration in which palmettes (often arranged following the in-and-out design), lanceolate leaves, and frequently also cloudbands dominate, both because of their size and their chromatic contrast with the deep red ground, which is enlivened by smaller floral elements linked together by slender arabesques and plant tendrils; on rare occasions birds and small animals may also appear, but always in the background. The edges, generally very dark in colour and of an indeterminate shade somewhere between blue, green, and black, are normally decorated with *herati* borders, which is to say large flowers or palmettes often

Carpet with floral decoration; northeastern Persia (Herat?), end 16th-early 17th century. These carpets are characterized by red fields and dark borders, and their decoration is dominated by palmettes of various shapes and sizes. Each element is tied to the others by the inevitable continuous arabesque.

accompanied at the side by large lanceolate leaves.

Floral carpets, which originated at the end of the 16th century, enjoyed great success and became so widespread that their place of origin cannot be established with any degree of certainty. Examples of the type were thus once all attributed to Isfahan, but the tendency nowadays is to attribute them to Herat. In both cases, however, these are purely convenient commercial names, and other centers of production cannot be excluded.

Herat has been credited with the creation of one of the decorative elements found most frequently in these carpets, namely the *herati,* which was initially composed of a palmette (or rosette) accompanied only by two large, curving leaves with serrated edges. This early design provided the basis for the famous motif known as the field herati or simply *herati,* like the original prototype, numerous variants of which became common in carpets made throughout Persia during the 19th and 20th centuries.

The attribution of floral rugs is further complicated by the so-called Indo-Isfahan or Indo-Persian carpets, which were woven in India using the Persian floral design. These carpets prove the spread of the style to India, but it is extremely difficult to

Below: This diagram presents the prototype from which the famous herati *motif descended. It is composed of a central floral element surrounded by two characteristic serrated curving leaves.*

Bottom: Polish medallion carpet; central Persia (Kashan?), 17th century. The use of gold and silver threads, the coarse knotting, and the floral decoration

without the usual Persian calligraphic sensibility are the elements that characterize these carpets, which were made for export.

distinguish a Persian floral carpet from an Indian example made in the same design. The Persian carpets display a greater calligraphic quality, emphasized by the dark outlining of the figures, and a more pronounced taste for strong colours, while the figures of Indian carpets have either pale outlines or no outlines at all, a background normally of the charcteristic lac-dye red colour, and a generally less powerful quality. As might be guessed, the floral type, made from the end of the 16th century until well into the 18th century, became one of the most successful patterns in the Safavid repertoire. Rediscovered in the 19th century, it is still one of the most widely copied antique patterns today.

Polish or "Shah Abbas" carpets

Numerous carpets, scattered through the major European collections, have come to be called Polish or Polonaise because they share the same stylistic features as those from the collection of the Polish Prince Czartorysky that were displayed at the 1878 Paris International Exhibition. For this reason, and also because some of them are decorated with the coats-of-arms of the Polish nobility, they were once thought to have been made in Poland, when in reality

they were specially made in Persia.

These carpets are characterized by three main

features: the precious nature of their materials (silk, with areas of particular decorative importance enriched with gold and silver thread), their fairly wide range of decorative motifs (arabesques, flowering tendrils, palmettes, and cloudbands, either distributed full field or arranged around a single central medallion or repeating medallions), and the general delicacy of their

PERSIA

Portuguese carpet; southern Persia (?), 17th century; 145 x 265 inches. Bright and elaborate, these carpets are easily recognized because of their singular corner decorations of nautical scenes with people dressed in European clothes and large ships, as shown in the diagram at bottom.

colours, in which yellow, pink, sky blue, and pale green predominate. This elegance, however, is matched by somewhat shoddy, unoriginal decoration, and diminished calligraphic sensitivity. Such characteristics indicate that these carpets were special orders, made from the outset for distant and inexpert customers, and thus for export, but not as commercial products, since their undeniable preciousness indicates that they were not intended for the commercial market, but were made to serve as sumptuous and impressive presentation pieces reserved for the leading European courts. Their creation and their diplomatic functions were conceived during the reign of Shah Abbas the Great, for which reason they are also more justifiably referred to as Shah Abbas carpets. Produced from the end of the 16th to the end of the 17th centuries and known in Europe from the beginning of the 17th

century, these carpets have been attributed to the weavers of Kashan and Isfahan, but there is great controversy regarding the differences between the products of these centers.

Portuguese carpets

The name of these carpets is purely conventional, although it does indicate a very particular kind of decoration that is distinct from all the other carpets made under the Safavids. These are ordinary central-medallion carpets, thick with arabesques and tiny animals, but they are characterized by figural corners depicting nautical scenes with waves, fish, swimmers, and most of all large ships aboard which are visible captains, sailors, and passengers, all in European dress. The presence of these Western figures led to the theory that the carpets were made in the Indian city of Goa, an ancient Portuguese colony, and this gave the type its name. Their character is so unique with respect to the rest of the Safavid production of the same period that it has been suggested that the Portuguese commissioned them for sale in Europe and had them made in Goa or in the factories of southern Persia, an area where the Portuguese had commercial dealings in the 17th century. In any case, whether Goa or southern or even northern Persia, the provenance of these examples remains obscure. These singular carpets, large and lively, are all datable to the 17th century. Their decoration served as inspiration in the 19th century for carpets made in the Tabriz workshops.

Old carpets

After the 18th-century crisis marked by the Afghan invasion in 1722 and the long subsequent period of political and cultural eclipse, the art of the Persian carpet began a rebirth during the second half of the 19th century with the reopening of old workshops and establishment of new ones. In some cases workshops were opened at the instigation of Western interests, as was the case with the Ziegler workshops of Tabriz and Sultanabad, inaugurated in 1883. Most of the somewhat numerous examples of old Persian carpets were made in these famous city workshops; a limited number were made by nomadic populations.

City production

Old city-made Persian carpets are characterized by

PERSIA

Kashan prayer rug; 19th century. Imported from Anatolia, the Persian prayer rug is distinguished by its highly elaborate mihrab and lush naturalistic decoration.

colours, which are never garish, and, most of all, they pay the typical attention to the design and line, with the consequent use of black outlines around the figures. The prevalent style is clearly curvilinear or floral, but with the differences among production areas it is not at all rare to find geometric interpretations of both the abstract and stylized types.

The layout most used, so much so as to constitute the most representative of Persian carpets, is the central medallion, especially petallike, ogival, or round, resting on a background thickly covered with arabesques and spread with palmettes, leaves, flowers, and often various kinds of real or imaginary animals. Other successful layouts include those of hunts and animals and layouts with superimposed medallions and various motifs repeated in rows and enclosed in a full-field grid. Prayer rugs were also made, characterized by mihrabs shaped like curved arches occupied by naturalistic floral decorations, but prayer rugs were made only in limited numbers and usually to satisfy Western demand, since the prayer rug is an imported form in Persia, where the carpet has always had more of an artistic and social function than religious. The vast panorama of the decorative

the more or less faithful reproduction of the layouts and decorations of the magnificent Safavid period, which is taken as "classical." This reproduction was part of a general revival of the glorious past following the brief interlude of decadence, but it was also designed to satisfy the growing demand on the Western market. For this

reason, although city examples are not without value, they are partly debased by the absence of particularly original creations and further weakened by their increasing subjection to commercial needs. They present the overall lyrical and balanced character of antique carpets and employ the same wide range of

Senneh carpet with
full-field herati
decoration; 19th
century. Of all the
many decorative
motifs, the herati,
together with the
boteh, became the
most commonly used

element in Persia
beginning in the 19th
century. In various
forms it is used for the
ornamentation of
borders or fields and
sometimes both, as is
the case in this
example.

motifs, translated in geometric or curvilinear forms, includes the *mina khani*, the zel-i-sultan, the *kharshang*, the Afshan, the *boteh*, introduced to the decoration of carpets in the 18th century for the ornamentation of both fields and borders, and the *herati*, which was descended from the simpler 16th-century prototype and probably codified in the 18th century for use in the field, in the complex system of flowers and curling leaves arranged around a rhomboidal figure. For border decoration, the forms most often used, aside from the *boteh* and the *herati*, are cartouches and *medachyls*.

Two Westernized types

At the end of the 19th century two carpet types directly influenced by Western taste and culture came into production and met with moderate success. The first type was carpets with figural compositions. Most of these carpets present scenes of mythological events drawn from the literature of the Persian epics or heroic episodes taken from Persia's national history, but there are also carpets with bizarre scenes of hunting or daily life or portraits of important public figures or even wealthy commissioners of carpets. The borders are usually decorated with

cartouches containing various inscriptions and poetic verses, but in some cases lengthy blocks of text are written within the field to explain the scene depicted.

The scenes depicted clearly reveal the influence of Persian miniatures, but also evident is the influence of Western engravings, prints, and photographs, for the scenes show an obvious attempt at realism, primarily in terms of the background scenery, and as the figures depicted stand out because

of their size and importance in relation to the rest of the composition.

Thus at the end of the 19th century the human figure first appeared as the leading element in carpets, no longer woven into the intricate arabesqued backgrounds but placed within true pictorial scenes. Even so, because the geometric nature of the knotting technique made it impossible to achieve a fully realistic effect and, more importantly, because of the complete foreignness of

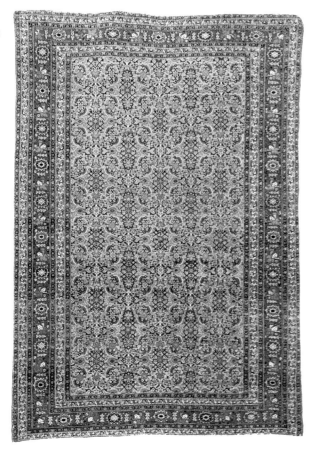

pink in all its shadings. Senneh was one of the leading centers of this production.

Nomad carpets

In Persia as elsewhere the carpets made by nomads remained tied to the traditional tribal life and immune to the commercial temptations presented by both the domestic and export markets. For this reason, after many years of strong prejudices against their ingenuous spirit and incessant attention paid instead to city-made examples, Persian nomad carpets are today the subject of ever-increasing interest. Strongly characterized by abstract or stylized geometric designs, old Persian nomad carpets can be distinguished from the tribal carpets made in other areas by their compositions, which are in general more dense and elaborate, often a result of the influence of city motifs. As with other tribal carpets, however, the colours are lively and contrasting; a case apart are the Baluch carpets, which stand out for their use of particularly dark and gloomy tints.

The provenance of Persian nomad carpets cannot be established with precision and remains an ongoing unresolved problem. This is primarily a result of the vastness of the territory in

these subjects to the purest decorative traditions of the carpet, these carpets are of a truly singular style, one that is not always appreciated or even liked. Among the various centers that distinguished themselves in the application of this style were Kashan and Kerman.

The second 19th-century type took its inspiration from 18th-century French floral decorations, which were transferred to carpets as large compositions of roses, peonies, and other flowers in a naturalistic style, gathered in bouquets or in luxuriant patterns. These carpets are distinguished by their colours, which are pastel tints with a certain predilection for light green, beige (especially for the grounds), and most of all

Below: Bakhtiari medallion carpet; end 19th century. Always characterized by abstract or stylized geometric designs, the carpets made by Persian nomads show more of the influence

of the elaborate city carpets than do nomad carpets made elsewhere.

Bottom: Tabriz medallion carpet; 19th century. The layout and type of floral decoration, descended from antique Safavid examples, are characteristic of this production area.

which the carpets were made and the close proximity of other important areas of production and exchange, such as Anatolia, the Caucasus, and Turkestan. For this reason, nomad carpets are not attributed to any specific group or village but are instead referred to by the name of a major tribe or the region in which the tribe lived.

Major production areas

Unlike carpets made by nomads, those made in artisan workshops in cities can be grouped into production areas based on their stylistic and technical characteristics. The numerous and varied carpets produced in Persia, both city and nomad, can be divided by the large geographic areas that include specific regions and centers.

The major production areas and the most-representative types of Persian carpets made in them, are the following.

PERSIA

Tabriz figural carpet; 19th century. This area boasts the production of a group of figural carpets with somewhat lively scenes, as in this case. A particular element is the main border, decorated with a continuous series of scenes.

Northwest Persia

Tabriz. The ancient production center of Tabriz initiated the 19th-century revival of Persian carpet making. Tabriz carpets are distinguished by the use of the symmetrical knot (the asymmetrical was in use during the Safavid period), the use of particularly coarse, strong wool, and by the habit of trimming the pile to a medium-low height.

Tabriz carpets are characterized by outstanding refinement in the workmanship, particularly evident in examples made in silk. These carpets stand out stylistically for their particular attention to detail, although the decorative schemes are rarely original, being descendants of antique classical layouts. The central medallion layout, with fractions of equal medallions in the corners, is the most used, but there are also vase designs, animal designs, and even Ghiordes-type prayer rugs; a small minority is composed of various types of figural scenes. The borders are usually decorated with *herati*, cartouches with inscriptions, and cloudbands; typical of Tabriz are narrow outer guards with small floral motifs. The predominant colours used are; blue, ivory,

and brick red, along with Western-style pastel tints.

Heriz. There is no doubt that Heriz has an ancient tradition of carpet making (although solid proof is lacking), and the town is known for its 19th-century

production of wool carpets, which are unmistakable not only for their symmetrical knotting and squarish shapes, but for their style. These carpets are characterized by the translation of classical Persian floral motifs into

Heriz medallion carpet; 19th century. Carpets from this area can be recognized easily by their geometric style, typical starlike medallion with four or eight points, and borders usually decorated with a stylized version of the herati. The design emphasizes the singular shape of the central medallion (shown in the diagram).

geometric forms whose designs are usually highlighted by two or more different-coloured outlines. The layout employed most often is based on a large central medallion in a starlike form composed of four or eight points, accompanied by geometric motifs on the sides. The borders are decorated with *herati* rendered in geometric forms and often transformed into the "turtle" motif, or with small variously composed polygons. Also typical is the way of using the colours, which are spread over large areas, unlike all other Persian carpets; the tints used most often are rust red, ivory, light yellow, blue, and light blue. Heriz also had a small production of

carpets in silk, but these have a commercial character, since they are decorated with more classical floral motifs or are made following the rules of the traditional curvilinear style. Most are prayer rugs with elaborate niches that are occupied by complicated floral elements and trees of life.

Area of Karadagh. Because it borders the Caucasus, this area of nomad and seminomad production is problematic. Karadagh carpets are characterized by their long formats and symmetrical knotting, making them stylistically similar to carpets from the nearby Caucasus. Their geometric-type decoration is usually based on several aligned medallions or a single central medallion always set against a ground spread thickly with small polygons or geometric plant elements. The main borders are usually decorated with the serrated leaves typical of the Caucasus, octagonal stars, or stylized floral vines. The ground colours are particularly dark, usually blues or browns,

PERSIA

Senneh carpet with full-field boteh *decoration; end 19th-early 20th century. This production area is distinguished by minute designs arranged in orderly rows across the entire* field. *Aside from* boteh, herati *are also used a great deal.*

while the medallions and principal designs are rendered in more lively colours, such as red, ivory, yellow, and blue.

Western Persia

Senneh. Senneh carpets attracted attention in Western markets early on because of the high density of their knotting, and the name of this center has come to be used for the asymmetrical knot, which is ironic because since Senneh carpets have always been made using the symmetrical knot. Thanks to particular technical skills used during the knotting and to the trimming, which is always low, these carpets stand out for their meticulous full-field designs. In most cases these are tiny *herati* or *boteh* in repeating rows; in some cases the *herati* are presented within central hexagonal or rhomboidal medallions, which are often concentric, or within aligned medallions. At the end of the 19th century new decorations reflecting Western taste came into use, characterized by French-style bouquets of flowers. The main borders usually bear *herati*. The predominant ground colours are blue, black, and ivory, while the designs are made in yellow, red, light green, and cream.

Bidjar. Made using the symmetrical knot, Bidjar carpets appear in a wide variety of designs, from central medallions to *mina khani* to *kharshang*. They are distinguished by their rigid and rectilinear translations of classical Safavid decorations, especially of the vase layout, arabesques, and floral vines. The colours are always contrasting: decorative motifs in bright tints, such as red, blue, yellow, and green, stand out against darker grounds.

Area of Hamadan. Because of their technical and stylistic characteristics, the carpets from this production area are easy to recognize.

Made using the symmetrical knot, Hamadan carpets are trimmed high and have a compact structure obtained by alternating a single pass of the weft for every row of knots. The most common layouts are those with a medallion or superimposed medallions; the rhomboidal or hexagonal shape of the medallion is also characteristic, and the medallion is usually completed by two pendants, and its interior is often decorated with geometric *herati*. The general language of these carpets is geometric and linear, so the borders are usually decorated with polygonal elements or stylized plant elements; there is almost always a *medachyl* border, aside from an outer guard that is camel colour, also the usual colour for the ground of the field.

Area of Malayer. Malayer is a complex zone: the north gravitates stylistically toward Hamadan, with square medallions and small full-field motifs; the east gravitates toward the style of Sarouk and Ferahan, with more elaborate central-medallion layouts and larger and more complex floral decorations. The language is consistently geometric, although both symmetrical and asymmetrical knots are used. Floral designs, particularly the zel-i-sultan,

PERSIA

Below: Malayer medallion carpet; 19th century. The floral design, similar to the Sarouk and Ferahan styles, indicates that the carpet was made in the area east of Malayer. The geometric forms are a constant in these carpets.
Bottom: Malayer medallion carpet; 19th century. The large geometric medallion and the rigid and dense interpretation of the herati motif indicate that the carpet was made in the area north of Malayer.

are used a great deal, distributed full field or alternating with rhomboidal medallions. The colours are lively, with a preference for red and blue.

Area of Ferahan. Made in most cases using the asymmetrical knot, the carpets from this area can be divided into two types. The first usually has a full-field decoration of floral motifs based on Persian originals, first among them tiny geometric *herati*. The second is characterized by a well balanced medallion layout: the medallion, often surrounded by jagged rays and filled with floral motifs, dominates the center. The rest of the field is somewhat bare, decorated with a few floral elements widely spread and by slight fractions of another two medallions located above and below the central medallion. Much appreciated in Europe this type is further characterized by the red or beige colour of the field.

Sarouk (or Sarough). This area's rugs, usually made using the asymmetrical knot, are easily recognized by their distinctive linear versions of such traditional Persian floral decorations as vines, leaves, and buds, which in these carpets seem stiffened, but are singularly effective. This highly original linear

Ferahan medallion carpet; early 19th century. The round medallion with its sunburst outline is accompanied by small fractions of two other medallions. The design of the border is the herati "turtle" (shown in diagram)

The pink of Sarouks

Colors have always been of great importance in the production of carpets in the village of Sarouk in central Persia. Indeed, for a certain period natural colouring substances were still being used in Sarouk after chemical dyes had been introduced almost everywhere else.
Typical of this production area is the use of a certain shade of very intense salmon pink, with blue reflections, called dughi, which is obtained by introducing a certain substance during the usual dyeing procedure. The base red colour is made, as is common in Persia and elsewhere, using the roots of madder, a plant that grows wild or is cultivated. Dried and pulverized, the roots are soaked in water and then yogurt (the dughi in question) or curdled milk is added to the mixture, these being substances that contain lactic acid, which yellows the fibers, also conferring shine and stability to the colours. At this point the threads are immersed in the dye for a few hours, then are rinsed for a long time and, once dried, are tinted a perfect dughi pink. This colour attracted particular attention in the United States market beginning at the end of the 19th century; for this reason, between the close of the 19th century and the first years of the 20th great numbers were made for export to America and came to be known as American Sarouks. To make the carpets even more pleasing to that market, the dughi pink ground is not enlivened by the geometric-style designs typical of the area but by floral decorations (bouquets or flowering vines across the entire field or forming a central medallion), which are of a naturalistic taste translated in the curvilinear style.

Sarouk prayer rug;
end 19th century.
Applied to prayer
rugs, the linear style
of Sarouks transforms
trees and flowers into
rigid forms that are
just as appealing.

character began slowly transforming itself into more curvilinear and naturalistic forms during the last years of the 19th century. The layout most often used is the central medallion, which can be very large and hexagonal or smaller and round or rhomboidal, with pendants and spandrels. Sarouk carpets can also use floral decorative elements or the prayer-rug layout. The borders are usually decorated with stylized *herati*, often transformed into the "turtle" motif. The colours, usually very pleasant, have found much favour on the Western market. The ground of the field is usually ivory, beige, red, or blue; the remainder of the decorations are usually yellow, blue, brown, and a typical shade of pink known as *dughi*.

Serabend. Carpets from this area, rarely knotted with the symmetrical system, can be easily recognized by their singular decoration. They are characterized by a preference for full-field layouts, composed exclusively of regular rows of tiny *boteh* all pointing in the same direction or in alternating rows pointing in different directions. In turn, the outlines of the *boteh* are rectilinear and continuous or discontinuous and formed of groupings of tiny flowers. The predilection for this

decorative motif probably led to the much-discussed name *boteh miri*, meant to indicate "the chosen, the best." Also characteristic of these carpets is the main border, formed of a typical vine with obliquely serrated leaves in which other *boteh* and floral elements are arranged. The ground of the field is always red, and the *boteh* and other designs are usually white, blue, black, or yellow.

Southwestern Persia

Luri. The carpets made by these nomadic and seminomadic peoples are problematic because of their variety. They are made using both symmetrical and asymmetrical knots and include examples decorated by grids, containing stylized plant elements, and with full-field decorations that are composed of tiny

121

PERSIA

Left: Serabend carpet with full-field boteh decoration; 19th century. Serabends are distinguished by their red ground, decorated with tiny boteh arranged in regular rows.

Right: Luri carpet with geometric decoration; early 20th century. The grid design and palette based on red and blue have been typical of these rugs since the beginning of the 20th century.

geometric motifs arranged in regular rows.

The colours used, originally somewhat bright and lively, began to grow darker at the beginning of the 20th century, with red and blue predominating.

Bakhtiari. The carpets made by this nomadic and seminomadic people are made with the symmetrical knot and are primarily characterized by what has been called the "Bakhtiari" pattern: the field is regularly divided in rows of squares, octagons, or diamonds each of which contains stylized plant motifs (trees, bushes, and flowering branches). The colours used most often are blue, red, yellow, and green.

Central Persia

Veramin. Although this production area came into existence during the 19th century and thus has no ancient carpet-making tradition, it is associated with one particular design. Made using the asymmetrical knot, Veramin carpets are distinguished for their characteristic full-field decoration using the *mina khani* motif, a floral grid of obscure origins. The main border is usually decorated with *herati*, often stylized and transformed into the "turtle" motif. The colours are those codified by tradition elsewhere; blue is used for the ground of the field, while white, red, yellow, and blue are the basic tints for the floral decorations.

Below: Bakhtiari medallion carpet; end 20th century. These carpets are distinguished by the "Bakhtiari pattern," composed of regular rows of polygons bearing stylized plant motifs.

Bottom: Detail of a Veramin carpet with full-field mina khani decoration; early 20th century. The type of floral decoration, herati border, and colours are typical elements of this production area.

Kashan. An ancient center of Safavid production, Kashan is still one of the best known and most appreciated production areas. Thickly knotted using the asymmetrical system and distinguished by the use of at least one weft strand coloured blue, these carpets show inspiration drawn from ancient designs and classical decorations. They are characterized by a marked preference for the central-medallion layout. This medallion, polylobate but of a variable form, is usually enriched by pendants and corner elements and rests on a field dense with arabesques and studded with palmettes, leaves, and other plant elements, often interspersed with small birds and other animals. Less frequent are full-field layouts, and these are always decorated with floral or zoomorphic motifs. The small-size rugs made here include prayer rugs, which usually have a pale ground and are decorated with the tree of life, flowering vases, and animals. Around the end of the 19th century figural scenes appeared, characterized primarily by the depiction of ancient Persian legends. Representation of the fabled "waq-waq" tree came back into use during those years, but it was usually transformed into a full-field tangle of vines, ending in

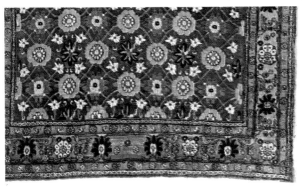

123

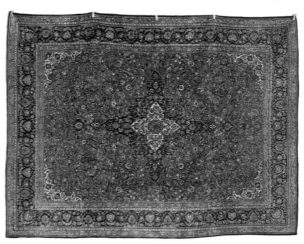

the heads of animals or monsters.

Applied to carpets in this area the curvilinear style becomes distinctly soft and flowing, although it was slightly more angular and stylized in some examples from the period before the introduction of more naturalistic forms. The borders have a wide variety of floral designs, always of Safavid inspiration, such as compositions using vines, flowers, and palmettes. The many colours usually permit contrast between the light, brilliant colours of the field and the darker tones of the main border, which were most often woven in dark blue. The ground of the field is almost always red or ivory; the decorations are in pastel tints. Around the end of the 19th century these vivacious tonalities began to dim, beginning with the borders, which became gray, beige, ivory, and pink.

Joshaghan. An ancient center of carpet production under the Safavids, Joshaghan has been credited with the creation of the vase design, although many doubts surround the attribution. Joshaghan carpets, made with the asymmetrical knot, are datable to the 18th century and most often appear with one of two representative types of decoration, both stylizations of the Safavid vase design. In the first type, small flowers are inserted in a grid layout formed by their stems; over time, the grid became increasingly stylized until it disappeared completely during the second half of the 19th century, by which time it was merely suggested by the diamond arrangement of the groups of flowers. In the second type, the grid is formed by the elongated and stylized leaves from yet another version of the *herati* motif, it too accompanied by small flowers. The borders contain stylized floral elements and usually have blue or ivory grounds, while the field is usually dark red with blue, light blue, white, or yellow decorations.

Southern Persia

Region of Fars. Carpets from this vast region are also called Shiraz carpets, after the name of the market city where they were gathered for sale. In reality, they were made by two large nomadic populations, the Kashkai and the Khamseh, but since the characteristics of the carpets made by the two groups are so similar that one cannot be distinguished from the other with any certainty (in particular with 19th-century examples), they are usually referred to more generally by the name

of the region. Almost always made with the asymmetrical knot, these carpets usually have a central medallion layout with a rhomboidal medallion, or a superimposed-medallions layout with several rhomboidal medallions. The field is most often covered by small geometric elements (various polygons, eight-pointed stars), plant motifs (rosettes, vines), or highly stylized animals, such as the

The morghi motif

Since it depicts a domestic animal in a rigorously geometric style, this decorative motif is eminently typical of nomad carpet production. The word morghi means "hens," and that word could be used as the name for this motif since it consists in the representation of small multicolour hens depicted in profile while busy pecking. This motif is characteristic of the nomad production of southern Persia, in particular the region of Fars inhabited by the Afshari people. In these examples the stylized hens appear multiplied in rows across the entire field in very small sizes, arranged around one, two, or three rhomboidal medallions or even within the medallions; sometimes, especially in Khamseh carpets made in Fars, four hens of a slightly larger size appear inside one or three medallions arranged in pairs that face each other across the longitudinal axis of the carpet (diagram below). The paternity of this singular motif has been the source of much discussion but is still unresolved: some scholars hold that it should be attributed to the Afshars, others believe that it was invented by a certain Arab Khamseh tribe living in the region of Fars. Unfortunately the scarcity of available examples does not yet permit resolution of the question.

"hens" called morghi, which also appear in the Afshar nomadic carpets. The influence of Safavid art shows up in more articulated medallions and the introduction of several more composite decorative motifs, such as arabesques and floral vines, always translated in the geometric style. Characteristic and frequently encountered is the use of narrow borders decorated with multicolour panels located along the short sides of the carpet, outside the usual borders. Superficial distinctions can be made between the carpets made by the region's two nomadic groups. In general, Kashkai carpets display a greater tendency toward the curvilinear and a more obvious preference for dark colours compared to the brighter colours and more linear style of Khamseh carpets. Characteristic of both groups is the frequent appearance, in somewhat ingenuous and stylized forms, of the lion, an animal that once inhabited the area and that represents the symbolic attributes of strength and domination.

Afshar. The name of the leading tribe in the region is usually used to indicate the carpets made by nomadic or seminomadic peoples in the area south of Kerman. Made using either the symmetrical or the

asymmetrical knot, these carpets have greatly varying decoration, since some were made following tribal traditions while others were influenced by the ornamental motifs of carpets made in nearby city workshops. Thus cruciform medallion layouts or rhomboidal superimposed-medallion layouts appear on fields spread with small floral elements and stylized animals and exist side by side with layouts and motifs foreign to tribal tradition, such as small floral medallions, *kharshang*, and frequently *boteh* (often in the stylized "mother-and-

son" version). These motifs borrowed from the city workshops are repeated in rows across the field. Also found are more elaborate layouts, taken from the decorative traditions of city workshops. Characteristic of these nomadic carpets is the *morghi* motif, shared with the region of Fars, which is composed of small stylized hens usually distributed in narrow rows located around a central rhomboidal medallion or around the several rhomboidal medallions of superimposed-medallions layouts. The borders are usually decorated with stylized

rosettes or rosettes on vines. The colours tend to contrast dark backgrounds, usually blue, and paler or brighter decorations in red, white, yellow, or green, although black is also used.

Kerman. A famous and ancient center of Safavid production, where the vase technique as well as the vase design were probably born, Kerman is today one of the most popular carpet provenances. Its carpets are easy to recognize both for their technique and style. Made using the asymmetrical knot, Kermans have three passes of weft for

Left: Kerman Ravar medallion carpet; 19th century.

Right: Kerman prayer rug; 19th century. Kerman prayer rugs are distinguished not only by the inclusion of realistic flowers and animals, but most of all by the transformation of the

tree of life into long linear plants forming a continuous floral arabesque.

Kerman Ravar

The name Kerman Ravar, often corrupted into Kerman Lavar or Kerman Laver, comes from the language of the carpet trade and refers to the highest quality and most refined carpets—those of the highest standards—from the city of Kerman. The village of Ravar, located to the northeast of Kerman, boasts an ancient tradition of carpet making, although the stylistic characteristics of its antique carpets cannot be defined with any clarity, since they are blended together with those of the nearby and far more famous center. The only differences that can be made out are hardly significant and

have to do with the higher trimming of the pile and less curvilinear designs of Ravars. It should be remembered that the denomination Kerman Ravar does not refer to any true production area or to any style, but is only a purely conventional commercial term that has been adopted on the European market to define the most refined examples made in the city of Kerman and its environs. Kerman is often said to produce the most refined and elegant Persian rugs, and Ravar sets its highest standards, so a Kerman Ravar is a carpet of the highest quality.

every row of knots, and the middle weft strand is tinted pink in the oldest examples and blue in later carpets. These carpets are characterized by their extremely elaborate and complicated curvilinear style, which grew even stronger in examples from the late 19th century that incorporated tortuous *islim* motifs. This particular curvilinear design was used in a large variety of layouts, both from the Safavid tradition and from other traditions. Thus there are central polylobate medallions on fields thickly strewn with arabesques and naturalistic floral elements;

ree layouts (most often cypresses); grids of shrubs; full-field *boteh* or bouquets of flowers; prayer rugs decorated by realistic vases of flowers or trees of life; and figural carpets with hunting or various other scenes, often negatively influenced by Western taste. At the beginning of the 20th century central medallions with bunches of naturalistic roses, showing French influence, appeared.

Another almost constant characteristic is the numerous borders—usually five or seven are used, most often decorated with plant lines or small *boteh*. The colours are very varied,

finely balanced, and played out with measured areas of tonality; the dominant colours are various shades of red, beige, blue, or ivory for the field, and blue, pink, and green for the decorations.

Eastern Persia

Region of Khorasan. This vast territory, which once included the city of Herat, an important creative and manufacturing center during the Safavid era, boasts an ancient carpet-making tradition which originated the widely used *herati* motif. Its carpets, made using the

asymmetrical knot, stand out for a particular technical aspect: during the knotting four or more rows of weft are passed for every six to seven rows of knots, which produces a strange, grooved effect on the back of the carpet. The most common layouts are the central medallion (of a roundish or polylobate form), concentric medallions, or full-field decoration using closed *herati* or small floral decorations. The main border is normally decorated with *herati*, *boteh*, or cartouches. The favourite colours for the field are blue or red and, for the designs, yellow, green, and blue.

Khorasan medallion carpet; 19th century. These carpets can be recognized by their technical particularities, the round polylobate medallion, and the boteh border.

Right: Meshed medallion carpet; end 19th century. Characteristic are the round medallion and the individual pendants with pale grounds arranged in the corners.

Meshed. The finest carpets from the Khorasan region are commercially attributed to this city, although the entire region has a long tradition of carpet making. Meshed carpets date from the end of the 19th century and are made using the asymmetrical knot. The most common design is that of the medallion, normally round or elongated and embellished with pendants and decorated with floral elements. The field is adorned with *herati* or naturalistic flowers and palmettes; it frequently also involves the swirling coils of the *islimi* motif. The corners are decorated with single pendants with pale backgrounds (usually white or ivory), either pentagonal or almond-shaped, which are often linked to the central medallion by *islimi* motifs or arabesques. These singular pendants represent one of the distinctive elements of this type. The main border generally displays the *herati* motif or floral vines. In general, the dominant colours are those found in other Khorasan carpets to which are added a special predilection for the use of an ivory white. A distinctive feature is the use in certain examples of the jufti knot, which originated in this region.

Baluch. The nomadic and seminomadic peoples living along the border with Afghanistan have given their name to this specific type of carpet. These carpets are often erroneously called Baluchistan carpets after the geographically nearby region, but they are totally unconnected to that region and are made by peoples who travel along the vast border region of Persia, Afghanistan, and Pakistan. Baluch rugs, which with few exceptions use asymmetrical knotting, are easily identifiable by their particular softness and more especially by their tendency to rely on a narrow range of rather dark ground colours, based on various shades of red, brown, and blue, which are lightened by the white, pale green, and

yellow of their designs; another singular feature is the use of a particular shade of aubergine purple. Because of their dark colouring, these rugs for a long time proved unpopular in the West and were considered of only restricted ethnographic interest, but today they are finally being reevaluated precisely because of their typical and genuine character. Based on full-field decoration, Baluch carpets display influences derived from the decorative motifs of neighbouring regions such as rows of variously hooked, polygonal, or romboidal Turkoman-type *guls*) and from traditional Persian city-workshop carpets (such

as *herati* and *mina khani*, these naturally being translated into geometric versions). Another variety typical of Baluch are prayer rugs characterized by long, rigid mihrabs with squared arches generally containing two-coloured trees of life against a camel-colour background;

these trees are composed of a rectilinear trunk from which spread perpendicular branches embellished with stylized flowers or leaves. The main border of all Baluch carpets is generally decorated with geometric elements of varying size and shape.

PERSIA

 Antique carpets

 Later carpets

KASHAN (?)

Medallion carpet (Ardebil); 1539-1540. Typical: cartouche border and central medallion.

TABRIZ (?)

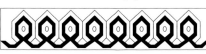

Hunt carpet; 1522-1523. Typical: border and hunting scenes.

TABRIZ

Figural carpet; 19th century. Typical: border and the dominant presence of human figures.

HERIZ

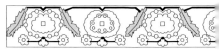

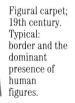

Medallion carpet; 19th century. Typical: border with geometric *herati* and starlike medallion.

HERAT (?)

Palmette
carpet; 16th-
17th century.
Typical: *herati*
border and
palmettes.

KERMAN (?)

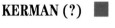

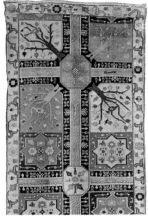
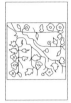

Garden carpet;
17th-18th
century.
Typical: border
and geometric
compartments.

SENNEH

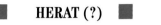

Carpet with
full-field
boteh; end
19th-early
20th century.
Typical:
border and
repeating
boteh.

SAROUK

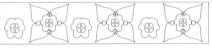

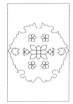

Medallion
carpet; 19th
century.
Typical:
border and
geometric
medallion.

PERSIA

■ Antique carpets

□ Later carpets

LURI

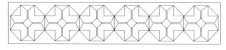

Carpet with geometric decoration; early 20th century. Typical: border with rosettes and geometric medallions.

BAKHTIARI

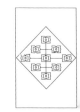

Medallion carpet; end 19th century. Typical: border and medallion with stylized flowers.

VERAMIN

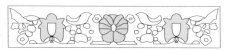

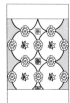

Carpet with full-field *mina khani*; early 20th century. Typical: border and motif repeated in field.

KASHAN

Medallion carpet; 19th century. Typical: border with *herati* and curvilinear medallion.

134

KASHKAI

Carpet with full-field *boteh*; end 19th century. Typical: border and particular design of the *boteh*.

KERMAN

Medallion carpet; 19th century. Typical: border with *herati* and curvilinear medallion.

MESHED

Medallion carpet; end 19th century. Typical: border and corner motifs.

BALUCH

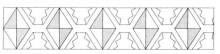

Prayer rug; 19th century. Typical: geometric border and the niche.

THE CAUCASUS

◆ Caucasian carpets are distinguished by their extreme and rigorous geometry, their marked inclination to abstraction, and their use of a few, particularly bright and contrasting, colours. Their decoration is based on elementary compositions using large or small polygons of all forms but not very complex, such as octagons, hexagons, and rhombuses, among which sometimes appear the figures of plants, animals, and even humans, but always highly stylized. The colours, spread over broad fields, are immediate and reveal a preference for contrast between cold colours and powerful reds.

The designs often show the influence of decorative motifs from Turkestan, Persia, and most of all Anatolia, and indeed there are often very strong expressive similarities between Caucasian carpets and those of Anatolia. Caucasian carpets can be distinguished from Anatolian carpets by their style, which is decidedly more archaic, simple, and lively, and always tends to abstraction. Caucasian knotting is exclusively symmetrical, with a medium density of knots. The material most often used is wool, which is employed both for the foundation and the pile; the pile is usually trimmed medium-high. The

formats are usually narrow and elongated, of medium to small size; however, antique Caucasian carpets are an exception, for they can be found in large sizes, although this is usually a matter of length. The compositional layouts most often used are

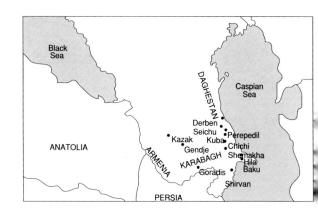

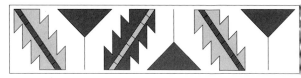

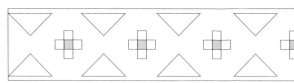

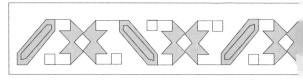

In the Caucasus only the symmetrical knot is used.

superimposed medallions (two or three medallions accompanied by secondary decorative motifs) and full-field decoration formed by the repetition of a single small geometric motif, abstract or stylized. Talish carpets form a category apart, for their field is entirely empty, with no decoration beyond the single ground colour.

Antique carpets

The ancient Caucasian populations most probably learned the technique of knotting from Seljuk invaders during the 11th century. No concrete proof of such original creations has survived, nor is there any pictorial record, and the oldest known examples from the area date to the 16th to 17th century and belong to a later artistic period, one that had already been influenced by the spread of the Persian floral style. This period lasted until the early 19th century and led to the creation of two complex carpet types, dragon carpets and floral carpets, both of which were made in large sizes by specialized workshops for wealthy buyers.

Dragon carpets

The first type is composed of the so-called dragon carpets, which stand out for their use of this legendary

animal in motifs repeated in the field. Dragon carpets are based on a grid layout in which the grid is formed by long, narrow, stylized leaves, in two colours, arranged so as to mark off large open rhomboidal spaces. Within these spaces are stylized dragons in the form of the letter S, as well as other fabulous animals, such as the phoenix and the chi'lin, an animal half dragon and

THE CAUCASUS

Dragon carpet; southern Caucasus, 17th century. Stylized dragons can be seen within the two upper and two lower diamonds. The diagram shows the even more stylized dragon that appeared in examples from the end of the 18th century.

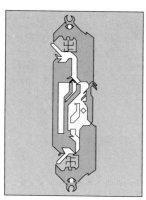

half deer, and even others, often unrecognizable. At the intersections of the leaves and sometimes also within other rhomboidal spaces are located palmettes and other flowers, all rigorously geometric. There are usually three borders, formed by a narrow main border variously decorated by two smaller, minor borders; the decorations vary a great deal and can be of geometric derivation or based on the Persian naturalistic style, such as vines formed of leaves and palmettes, rosettes, or small medallions, elements shaped like a horizontal S, and serrated leaves. The background colours are usually red, black, or blue, with the dragons and the other decorative motifs in ivory, yellow, and green. The production centers for these carpets, as well as the dating, remain somewhat obscure; they were at one time attributed to Armenia (for which reason these carpets are also called Armenian) or to the area of Kuba, while today they are more generically attributed to the region of Karabagh, an area in the southern part of the Caucasus known for its rich creation and the diffusion of its carpets.

Floral carpets

The second type of antique Caucasian carpet production, which also developed through the influence of Persian carpets, is floral carpets. These appear in a great variety of designs, but all of them lead back to three basic compositions. The first and oldest presents the same type of grid structure as the dragon carpets, but in place of those mythical animals uses stylized palmettes and variously articulated cruciform medallions. The second composition, probably datable to the 18th century, was created through a process of stylization and enlargement of the grid layout; it is characterized by the disappearance of the grid and the expansion of the medallions, which, assuming a sunburst form with a pale ground and alternating with large, highly stylized floral elements, are arranged vertically on the central axis in imitation of the superimposed-medallions layout. The third composition is distinguished by the full-field distribution

of tiny geometric elements of floral origin, all densely joined one to another by stems and arabesques. Among the various designs in the third group are combinations of palmettes, of clear Persian derivation from Herat or Isfahan, and articulations on three vertical axes, always with in infinite repetition, of Afshan motifs (with the typical forked plant element) or *kharshang* (with the characteristic zoomorphic palmette). The floral type, once generally attributed to the production area of Kuba, is today attributed in a broad sense to the southern Caucasus.

The 19th century and the new geometric-abstract style

The beginning of the 19th century was a period of fundamental importance for the Caucasian carpet, for its development was then favoured by particular historical circumstances. The Russian occupation that began early in the century brought the end of the ancient Caucasian nobility, and with it also the end of the production of large-size carpets made for the court. With the decline in the influence of the Persian floral style and the closing of the great specialized

THE CAUCASUS

workshops, the simpler, local production of small villages experienced a rebirth. This production had evidently never been dormant, even though no antique examples exist today, and it now found itself in a favourable position to best express the true geometric-abstract spirit of the Caucasian peoples. The new geometric style, rigorous and lively, blended the atavistic tribal spirit with the ancient Seljuk tradition and the decorative motifs drawn from the great period of court production by way of a process of enlargement and rarefaction. Therefore this was not a period of regression, moving from advanced forms to more primitive ones, but an important moment of rediscovery of original roots and thus of expressive growth.

It can thus be said that the true Caucasian carpet came into being in the 19th century and has come to stand apart from the carpets made in other production areas for its simplicity, immediacy, maximum tendency toward the abstract, vivaciousness of colours, and most of all for its general impression of being at the same time both archaic and stately.

Nineteenth-century Caucasian carpets can be recognized by their compositional and decorative simplicity, based on the relationships among decorative elements that are primary, secondary, or used only to fill space. The fundamental layouts involve the arrangement of medallions along the central axis or according to the well-known "four-and-one" scheme; also very frequent are full-field layouts, created by the distribution of such small geometric motifs as Afshan, *kharshang, boteh, herati,* and *mina khani* or by tiny stylized floral elements, arranged in geometric grids. There are also prayer rugs, characterized by a mihrab just barely discernible, often indicated only by a geometric arch, and usually occupied by small- and medium-size decorative elements that extend full field. All the figures

*Shirvan prayer rug;
19th century.
Caucasian prayer
rugs can be recognized
by the geometric arch
only slightly outlined
and nearly lost in the
uniform full-field
decoration.*

employed are exclusively geometric in character: the primary and secondary medallions are octagonals, hexagonals, rhomboids, or cruciforms, all with variously shaped profiles: stepped, fringed, smooth, hooked, and so on. The motifs used to fill space are animals, florals, and rarely, very stylized humans, eight-pointed stars, horizontal-S forms, small polygons, and so on. There are usually three borders, composed of a principal border and two minor borders, all rigorously decorated with geometric motifs. The designs of the principal border vary a great deal and include the serrated leaf, arranged obliquely and alternating with tulips, the characteristic wavy design of the running dog, vines with stylized floral elements, kufesque motifs, various polygons, eight-pointed stars, horizontal-S motifs, and squares and rectangles with four hooks in imitation of the Turkoman *kotchanak* motif, as well as others. The colours are particularly lively and bright. The most commonly used are cold or neutral colours, such as blue, various tonalities of green, ivory, white, and black, arranged in telling contrasts with great quantities of red, yellow, and orange.

The new geometric and abstract style, decidedly strong, characterized all of Caucasian carpets during the 19th century and up to the beginning of the 20th century, with particularly intensive production. Around the end of the century, commercial needs brought on a thickening of the compositions, with a stiffening of the designs and a multiplication of the number of borders. The influence of Western taste and market demands also led to the creation of examples decorated with naturalistic flowers and roses of French derivation; the region of Karabagh and production centers in the eastern Caucasus were especially distinguished for production of this particular hybrid type of carpet.

Major production areas

Most of the examples of Caucasian carpets in existence today are datable to the second half of the 19th century. Organized in groups according to stylistic and structural similarities, they have been classified according to the geographic areas in which they were made, even though in many cases this is uncertain. The best known production areas, and thus the most popular types, are the following.

Kazak carpet with three medallions; 19th century. Typical of Kazaks are the medallions, which are often hooked, the rarefaction of the decorative elements, their abstract character, and the highly contrasting colours.

Kazak. Carpets known as Kazaks are the best known and most popular Caucasian carpets, but although the name Kazak is used a great deal in the commercial market, it does not indicate a place of production for these carpets, which were made not only in the city of Kazak but across a vast and imprecise area of the southwestern Caucasus. The origin of the name is uncertain, and it is used today to indicate a grade of quality in a group of carpets that share stylistic and structural similarities.

Kazak carpets can be easily recognized by their use of a limited number of imposing principal decorative elements, the size of which makes them dominate all the secondary decorations, which in turn are numerous but never either too dense or too small. Also typical of these carpets are the colours, which are strong and brilliant. The most frequent layouts are three aligned medallions; a single central medallion, which can be simple or arranged following the four-and-one scheme; and the full-field repetition of various medium or large polygons. The shape of the imposing geometric medallions varies a great deal, but they are always decorated inside by other smaller decorative motifs. The geometric shapes used most often in Kazak carpets are octagons, hexagons, rhombuses, swastikas, eight-pointed stars, and rectangles. A strange motif, somewhat reminiscent of a butterfly, is sometimes used for the principal medallions; known as a Sevan, from the place to which it is usually attributed, it is similar to a shield and probably descended from ancient heraldic motifs. The border designs are quite varied although most common are serrated leaves, geometric vines, multiform polygons, and repetitions of multicolour *kotchanak*. The colours used are few and

Kazak medallion carpet; 19th century. Examples of this type, characterized by a large central motif similar to a butterfly or shield, are also called Sevan, after a place of production.

The border decoration descended from the Turkoman kotchanak is frequently encountered.

ighly contrasting, ominated by pale and dark eds, intense blue, white, nd bottle green. Kazaks are atable to the mid 19th entury and early 20th entury. By convention, the ame Kazak is also applied o certain types of Karabagh arpets.

rea of Gendje. These arpets most certainly do ot come from the town of endje, a caravan stop iidway between Tbilsi and aku, or even from the urrounding area. The ame Gendje is a purely ommercial term applied to arpets of a uniform ylistic and structural type. he characteristics of this rpe are a not overly refined orkmanship and irticularly pale colours, redominantly white, ellow, light red, and blue. he designs are quite arious; some repeat the ecorations of Kazak arpets and stand apart om them by their more minous colours and ugher workmanship. One pe of decoration is typical Gendje carpets, however, d it reveals a certain eference for the rangement of small- or edium-size identical namental elements in ll-field diagonal rows. ows of identical geometric iteh, stylized flowers, ght-pointed stars, or small olygons are arranged side diagonal parallel

strips formed by contrasting colours. Sometimes the strips themselves are not used, in which in case the alternation of the colours of the various decorative motifs creates chromatic diagonal lines; the colours used show a strong predilection for yellow, blue, red, and white. The main borders usually have motifs of serrated leaves, small octagons, or stepped medallions; the minor

borders are usually decorated with *medachyls* in colours of blue-red and green-red.

Region of Karabagh or Karabakh. This traditional area of carpet production is probably where the antique dragon carpets were made. The 19th-century carpets from this region constitute a broad group united only by the use of certain very particular colours, such as a

143

Left: Detail of Karabagh carpet with floral decoration; mid 19th century. Called rose Karabaghs, these carpets can be recognized for their naturalistic decoration, *influenced by the French baroque. Right: Karabagh superimposed-medallions carpet; mid 19th century. Karabaghs of this type can be recognized by their particular* *colours, such as the pink tending to violet of this example.*

pink tending toward violet obtained with a dye of animal origin (using the cochineal insect instead of madder root, as is more common elsewhere) and various tonalities of green and yellow. The panorama of decorative styles is vast, but at least three stylistic groups can be distinguished. The first group includes carpets made in villages or among seminomadic groups that are characterized by traditional designs so similar to those of Kazaks that these carpets are

Below: Diagram
showing the typical
boteh of Goradis in
Karabagh; because of
the two large claw-
shaped leaves this
motif is also known as
the "scorpion" boteh.

Bottom: Karabagh
medallion carpet;
19th century.
Although this carpet
has Persian herati, its
contrasting colours,
border with serrated
leaves, and geometric
style indicate it was

made in the
Caucasus.

sometimes referred to as Kazaks for commercial purposes. The most frequent layouts are rows of polygons, hooked or not, arranged full field or layouts using two large medallions of various geometric shapes. Particular kinds of medallions are typical of this group. Two such medallions are those of the so-called cloudband Kazaks, also known as Chondoresks (so-named from their presumed place of origin), which are composed of two imposing octagons with interiors decorated with

bands of very thick and angular stylized clouds; and those of the eagle Kazaks, or Chelaberds, which are characterized by a typical sunburst form on a white background. An almost constant element of these Karabaghs, a decidedly traditional group, is the design of the main border, which is constituted of rows of eight-pointed stars, alternating red and blue on a white ground and joined by stylized legs that form octagonal spaces, each of which is occupied by a pair of tiny square leaves.

The second stylistic group includes city-made carpets showing Persian influence. These usually have full-field layouts with regular arrangements of *mina khani*, *herati*, and *boteh*, all interpreted in rigidly geometric versions. The style of the *boteh* evolved in the town of Goradis in Karabagh is a particular

case in point. The Goradis *boteh* is uniquely elongated and pointed and is accompanied by two curving leaves whose clawlike form gives the motif a shape reminiscent of a scorpion.

The third stylistic group, also composed of carpets made in cities, is easily recognized by the obvious influence of Western decorative motifs. At the beginning of the 19th century, the new Russian invaders commissioned the region's artisans to make carpets with decorative motifs in the French style. In this way a style was developed that initially achieved a good balance between foreign elements and the Caucasian spirit. These carpets, also known as Karabagh rose carpets, have geometric flowers arranged in garlands or bouquets and interspersed by stylized birds and various shapes of polygons. The

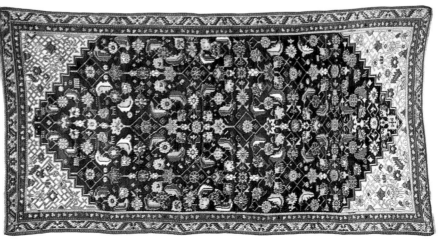

Talish carpet with full-field geometric decoration; 19th century. The narrow, elongated shape, small field in relation to the borders, and main border of large multicolour rosettes against a pale ground are all typical characteristics of this area. The interior of the field is often completely without decoration.

Chelaberds or eagle Kazaks

Chelaberd carpets are characterized by rows of two, three, and sometimes even four medallions of a particular shape. Each medallion is a cruciform polygon with extending rays; the medallions are blue or green and surrounded by a thick white line, and at their center is a smaller medallion against a red ground. In the usual composition, the three principal medallions are accompanied and completed by minor abstract or stylized geometric decorations spread across an invariably red field. The borders usually have the typical Karabagh motif, which consists of octagonal blue and red rosettes joined by geometric vines and forming in turn octagonal areas. The design of the medallions and their arrangement are derived from antique floral designs of rows of sunburst medallions. When a new type of Caucasian carpet

was designed in the 19th century, the procedure followed was that usually adopted in other areas: a single antique motif was chosen, extracted from its decorative context and enlarged, and then inserted together with new elements in new contexts. The design in question, which was probably symbolic originally, has various names. It is called the eagle or adler Kazak (adler is German for "eagle"), since the form of the medallion resembles the two-headed eagles used on noble coats of arms; sunburst Kazak since the design has a sunburst effect; and Chelaberd, from the town of Chelabi in the Karabagh region to which the type is attributed. There are many uncertainties about that attribution, however, and given the somewhat widespread use of this decorative element, it is better to refer it in general to several villages within the Karabagh region.

borders are usually decorated with geometric motifs; the colours tend toward pinks or reds for the flowers and dark blue or black for the ground. Around the end of the century, the production demands brought on by the great export market had an unfortunate effect on this carpet type, which lost its traditional spirit and became debased into realistic depictions of plants and animals rendered in less lively and contrasting colours.

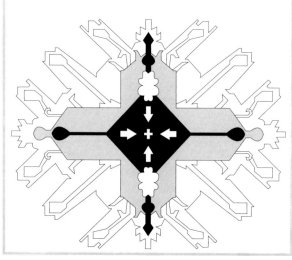

Region of Talish.

Talish carpets are quite easy to recognize because of their long, narrow shape and because of a quite singular aspect of their decoration: the long field is, in fact, usually completely empty, without any kind of decoration and occupied exclusively by a colour, usually dark blue and more rarely red. Only a running arrowhead motif, yellow or white, enlivens the internal perimeter of the field. Sometimes tiny geometric decorative motifs or stylized animals appear on the field, but only as widely scattered and isolated individual elements. In another type, however, the field is animated by orderly rows of small *boteh*, S motifs, eight-pointed stars, or elements of floral origin; in such cases, the dominant colours include light blue, yellow, and green. Also characteristic is the wide main border, almost always with a white ground, which is decorated with a typical motif of multicolour rhomboidal rosettes alternating with small geometric elements.

Area of Shirvan.

As is true in general of the carpets made in the eastern Caucasus, Shirvan examples are characterized by the diminished size of the decorative elements and their use in dense arrangements in which they

are separated by small areas of colour in a way that often gives a unique mosaic effect. The decorative variety of Shirvan carpets makes them stand out from the rest of Caucasian carpets, but this great variety can be divided into three basic layout types.

The first is a superimposed-medallions layout in which the medallions are of various geometric shapes and are accompanied by other elements—abstract or stylized, animal or plant—used to fill the open spaces. One such characteristic layout is composed of three to five hexagonal medallions with stepped outlines that are arranged on a dark blue field and joined one to another by thin segments; at each end of the row of medallions is a panel with a red background decorated with elements that are both abstract and stylized.

The second type has a full-field distribution of tiny decorative geometric floral motifs, either imaginary or of Persian origin, such as *boteh* and *mina khani*, arranged in rows or inside grids. The third type is composed of prayer rugs that have a blue or ivory ground and are characterized by small ornamental motifs in endless repetitions on which

THE CAUCASUS

Left: Shirvan superimposed-medallions carpet; 19th century. Typical of these carpets are the hexagonal medallions joined above and below by narrow, compressed segments and bordered at top and bottom by panels with red grounds.

Right: Hila medallion carpet; 19th century. Typical of these carpets are the field densely covered with multicolour boteh and the stylized floral vine along the outermost border.

the rectangular or pentagonal form of the arch of the mihrab is traced. The main borders of Shirvan carpets have serrated leaves, horizontal-S motifs, Kufic motifs, rosettes, *kotchanak*, and a unique design of hooked triangles of various colours. The ground colours are most often blue and yellow; the designs are in red, light blue, green, and white.

Area of Baku. Most carpets from the area of Baku are decorated with enlarged Afshan or *kharshang* motifs and are thus very similar to Kuba carpets. They differ from those, however, in terms of certain structural elements, particularly a preference for muted colours, such as ivory, blue, and light blue in all their tonalities. Characteristic of this area are the Hila (or Chila) carpets, which are named for a production center to the northwest of Baku, although there is no

148

Right: Chichi carpet
with full-field
medallion decoration;
19th century. The
main border with
rosettes and diagonal
bars is typical.

Bottom: Baku
medallion carpet;
19th century. The
colours and highly
stylized Afshan motif
are typical.

certainty that they were
made there. These carpets
are easy to recognize
because of their singular
decoration, which recalls
the medallion layout with
corner motifs of Persian
carpets. The field usually
has a dark blue ground and
is spread with multicolour
boteh arranged in rows or
set within a hexagonal grid.
On this field are arranged
one or three central
medallions, shaped like
stepped octagons, and four
corner motifs enlivened by
flowers, animals, or stylized
human figures. The main
borders usually have
rosettes, Kufic motifs, *boteh*,
and often small stylized
birds. In Hila carpets the
design of the outer guard
is typically characterized
by a pretty geometric floral
vine reminiscent of a
barber's pole.

Area of Kuba. The designs
most typical of Kuba involve
the enlargement of the
kharshang zoomorphic
palmettes and the corner
leaves of Afshan, which are
arranged with other floral
and abstract motifs, such as
medallions and rosettes.
These carpets are therefore
very similar to Baku carpets,

but they differ from them by
certain subtle technical
aspects, such as higher
trimming and a decidedly
more rich and lively palette.
Several other interesting and
widespread stylistic types
belong to this geographic
area and have been given the
names of villages or cities
near Kuba, even though
where they actually
originated is not absolutely
certain. The names of these
carpets thus indicate only
styles and designs.
    Chichi carpets are easily
recognized by their unusual
field and border designs. The
field usually has a dark blue,
black, or yellow ground and
is spread with hooked
octagonal medallions of
various colours in dense
rows that sometimes
alternate with geometric
flowers. The main border is
usually decorated with a

Below: Diagram of the Perepedil or "ram's horn" motif that distinguishes Perepedil carpets. Bottom: Seichur medallion carpet; 19th century. Typical are the "St. Andrew's cross" design of the field, the elaborate version of the running dog motif on the outer border, and the use of a colour between pink and brick.

singular motif, outlined in white on a blue ground, composed of octagonal rosettes alternating with diagonal lines.

Perepedil carpets can be easily distinguished by the presence in the field of a particular forked motif resembling a ram's horn, probably descended from ancient heraldic animal emblems. This motif, outlined in white, is usually arranged full field across a blue ground together with pale octagonal medallions with rosettes, geometric floral elements, and pairs of facing stylized birds located above and below each medallion. The main border is usually decorated with a Kufic motif in white on a blue or red ground.

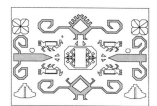

Seichur (or Zeichur) carpets can be recognized by various elements. First is the main border, decorated with a complex version of the wavy motif of the running dog coloured white and blue. Second is the use of a particular tone between pink and brick that is used both in the field and in the borders, often together with red. The fundamental element for recognizing these carpets, however, is a typical decorative motif found in the field: along the central axis of a dark blue or bottle-green field are spread several cruciform medallions from which extend four wide diagonal bars that form a characteristic X or "St. Andrew's cross," repeated to give a sense of endless repetition. These crosses form a kind of rhomboidal grid, the open spaces of which are decorated with minor geometric elements. In some Seichur carpets from the end of the 19th century, more or less stylized roses appear within this grid and along the main border, denoting the influence of French taste and marking the entry of this carpet type into the great commercial market of carpets made for export.

Region of Daghestan.
Carpets from this mountainous zone are distinguished primarily by their coarse manufacture and high-trimmed pile. From a stylistic point of view, there are no distinguishing motifs or unique layouts; the designs used are those common to other areas, but the way in which they are presented makes recognition of these carpets possible. In fact, although the decorative organization of Daghestan carpets is based on small ornamental motifs, as is true of the other production areas of the eastern Caucasus, the style is not very refined in its details, and the assemblies often seem sparse. Carpets with a notched grid containing abstract or stylized geometric elements on a white or blue ground are usually attributed to this region. This design is often imposed on prayer rugs, which are recognizable as such only by the arch of the mihrab, which is pointed or pentagonal. The name Daghestan is often applied to any prayer rug with a pale background, without differentiating the carpets of Shirvan, which are similar but are made with decidedly more care and refinement. Worthy of note are some Daghestan carpets of a naturalistic character from the end of the 19th century.

Caucasian soumaks

Aside from its knotted carpets, the Caucasus is also well known for the vast production of soumaks, pileless carpets made using the flatweave technique of wrapped weft threads. The name of this carpet type is most probably derived from a Caucasian center, the city of Shemakha, located to the east, near the Caspian Sea, but the technique is known and used not only in the Caucasus but throughout the entire Middle East. The antique Caucasian soumaks date to the early 19th century and are characterized by a particular attention to design and the use of a typical red colour, between rust and burnt, which is primarily used for the ground colour of the field. The decorative motifs are geometric designs based on the local repertory of decorative designs used for knotted carpets. The layout used most often is that of superimposed medallions, usually in the form of notched stars and usually coloured blue. Among the medallions and in the remainder of the field are other minor decorative elements, always of a geometric character, abstract or stylized, in lively colours, with a predominance of yellow, white, blue, and green. The borders are not always given a weight proportional to the design; among the most often employed designs are the running dog, more or less enlivened and stylized, rows of eight-pointed stars, and rosettes framed by octagons. Soumak carpets are compact and strong; they are almost always made entirely of wool; and their format, more or less elongated, can reach large sizes, with averages of 120-140 x 75-100 inches.

THE CAUCASUS

Antique carpets

Later carpets

◼ S. CAUCASUS ◼

Dragon carpet; 17th century. Typical: the floral border and dragon repeated across the field.

◼ S. CAUCASUS ◼

Floral carpet; early 18th century. Typical: border and full-field floral design.

◼ KAZAK ◼

Three-medallion carpet; 19th century. Typical: border with serrated leaves and large medallions.

◼ KARABAKH ◼

Medallion carpet; 19th century. Typical: border with serrated leaves and repeated *herati* motif.

TALISH

Carpet with geometric decoration; end 19th century. Typical: border with rosettes and field with arrowheads.

SHIRVAN

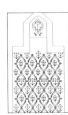

Prayer rug; end 19th century. Typical: border and niche only barely indicated.

BAKU

Medallion carpet; 19th century. Typical: border and repeating *boteh* in the field.

KUBA

Medallion carpet; 19th century. Typical: border and repeated small geometric medallions.

WESTERN TURKESTAN

♦ The carpet production of central Asia includes carpets made in two nearby but distinct geographical areas: western and eastern Turkestan. Carpets from western Turkestan are easy to recognize because of their singular style, which is rigorously geometric and abstract and based on designs and colours that have remained unchanged over the centuries and that are repeated as though part of a fixed code. The inevitable distinctive element around which the entire structure is built is decoration using *guls*, the Turkoman tribal emblems consisting of a usually octagonal medallion, the internal decoration of which varies in shape according to the tribe that made the carpet. These *guls* are reproduced in parallel rows across the entire field. The palette is decidedly limited, with red

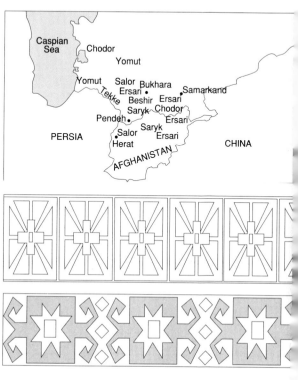

in all its tonalities predominating as the ground colour for fields and borders, and with blue, black, and white used for the designs. The decoration of the borders is essentially geometric-abstract, with the prevalence of polygonal designs and the typical *kotchanak* motif, displayed by two pairs of hooked elements. The general character that informs these carpets is one of simplicity. This does not mean, however, that the carpets are monotonous: their style is the fruit of an ancient tradition that has remained unchanged for centuries. This archaic

spirit, a descendent of ancestral symbols, has evolved, and any initial uniformity and banality has been transformed into an evocative expression of pride and strength. The knotting system used is primarily the asymmetrical type, with a very thick density of knots. Wool is usually the preferred material for both the foundation and the pile, but insertions of silk and natural cotton to make white-coloured areas are also found. The pile is usually trimmed to a medium-short height. The carpets vary in shape, running from long, narrow

Diagram of the asymmetrical knot, the most used in western Turkestan.

*Opposite: Map of
western Turkestan
showing the major
areas of production.
Typical borders of
western Turkestan:
cruciform designs
(above) and
.otchanak (below).*

*Below: Tekke carpet
with full-field* gul
*decorations; end 19th
century. The carpets
of western Turkestan
have maintained
their original
character unchanged.*

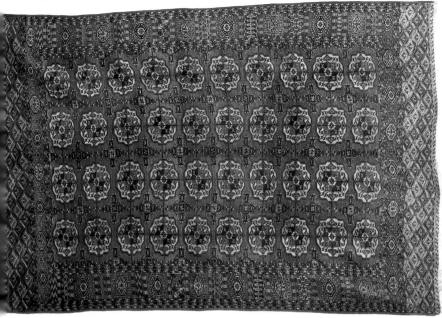

rectangles to squares, and the sizes are variable.

A singular style

In terms of carpet production, western Turkestan is usually taken to refer to a complex region, not at all geographically uniform, that includes Turkmenistan, Karakalpak, Uzbekistan, part of eastern Persia, and an area of northern Afghanistan. This zone is quite probably the area in which the technique of knotting carpets was born and from which it was spread by way of periodic migrations of people. In the new areas to which the technique spread the carpet underwent a process of evolution that from Anatolia to China transformed it into a product made for the courts of rulers; in western Turkestan, however, it continued to maintain its original significance as an object tied to the daily life, religion, and art of its people; the carpets from this region are the only ones to have preserved intact their original, exclusively nomadic, character.

Over the centuries, the nomadic and seminomadic Turkoman peoples have made their carpets following an ancient tradition that has remained faithful to itself in terms of both technique and style. These carpets are made by women and young girls who, working on rudimentary horizontal looms and using in most cases the asymmetrical knot, have perpetuated traditional designs and colours and employed decorative layouts that have been fixed and codified by the customs of each tribe and handed down orally from generation to generation. These carpets are geometric-abstract in style and use designs that resemble those of Anatolia and the Caucasus, as becomes clear when one examines the decorative motif that distinguishes the entire production area of western Turkestan: the *gul*. The *gul* medallion, usually octagonal (or hexagonal or rhomboidal), has contours of various shapes (hooked, polylobate, stepped, and so on) and has within it other small geometric figures. The decoration of Turkoman carpets is composed of the rhythmic repetition of *guls* in more or less thick parallel rows, sometimes joined one to another and often broken up by series of other minor geometric figures, such as rhombuses, starlike elements, and cruciform motifs.

The borders, most frequently composed of a main border and two minor borders, are decorated with abstract geometric elements, such as various polygons, horizontal-S motifs, frets, and the *kotchanak*. There is often a wider border on both short sides or, more often, on one side only. Each of the decorative motifs probably came into being from the stylization of a natural element (flower, bird, and so on) and without doubt once had a specific symbolic meaning, but today these meanings are lost and no longer recognizable. We still do not know if the *guls* came into existence as heraldic elements or if they developed from the simplification of complex central medallions that would have been difficult to reproduce in series. The palette, also codified by tradition, is limited and dark but enlivened in the grounds of the field and borders by the frequent use of reds; until the end of the 19th century this colour was obtained using madder, and it was later made using cochineal imported from

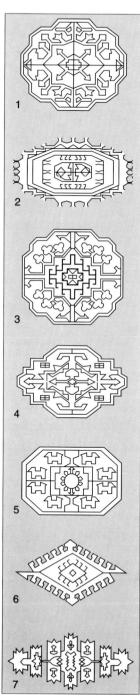

America. The other colours used for the designs are restricted to white, rendered using natural cotton, brown, black, orange, yellow, and to a lesser extent, blue and green.

Basing their activities and life itself on sheep husbandry and weaving, the populations of western Turkestan used the knotting technique to make not only large and small carpets, which served uses inside tents, but also many other objects of daily use, such as saddlebags of various sizes, sacks, cushions, trappings for their mounts, and tent door hangings. In this context, the carpet was looked upon as a valuable product to which was entrusted the cultural and artistic traditions of the tribe. The carpet thus represented a fundamental element in a wedding trousseau or funeral furnishing, but at the same time it remained a product necessary to the carrying out of life in every tent of the tribe. Because carpets were made to be used and therefore consumed, few early examples have survived and 17th-century specimens are rare; most of the carpets we have are datable to the beginning of the 19th century or later.

The decline

The carpets made in the early 19th-century show full

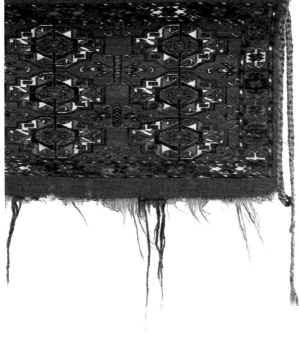

respect for traditions and always achieve high technical levels. This is not true of examples from the middle of the century. The rigidity and increased density of their designs as well as the diminished brilliance of the colours reveal the effects of both the penetration and consolidation of new commercial needs for overseas markets and the introduction of chemical dyes, which occurred here around 1880. Carpet making was also affected by the general decline of tribal society, a process that was hastened by the Russian conquest at the end of the century. Many people unjustly claim that the carpets made by the western Turkestan populations are rough and monotonous, but others have rediscovered and reevaluated them, finding that they represent a living and genuine attachment to ancient tradition, something that cannot be said of the sterile and purely imitative modern versions made in Pakistan and Afghanistan.

Major production areas

Carpets from western Turkestan are generically referred to as Bukharas or even Royal Bukharas, from the name of the city of Bukhara, which was, however, not a production area but a center of collecting and marketing carpets. Although the classification of carpets from western Turkestan presents many difficulties, these carpets can be grouped on the basis of style, which in this case means primarily on the basis of the various configurations taken by the *guls* in each tribe. The most important types identified using this system, referred to by the names of major tribes, are the following.

Tekke. This carpet type is characterized by the best-known Turkoman decoration, that which in the West has come to be referred to by the name Bukhara. It can be easily recognized since the field, usually red-purple, is covered by a thin black grid forming rectangular areas in which rows of equal-size *guls* are orderly arranged. Tekke *guls* can be recognized by their slightly compressed polylobate octagonal form, which is divided in four sections alternately coloured white/red and red/blue; in some of the oldest carpets the blue is sometimes replaced by green. The interior of the *gul* has a star motif from which spread minute diagonal designs resembling arrows that some people have taken for stylized floral elements and others for "eagle claws." These principal *guls*

Below: Tekke carpet with typical full-field decoration; 18th century. In this carpet, principal guls alternate with secondary gorbaghe guls across the characteristic Tekke grid.

Bottom: Diagrams of the two secondary Tekke guls: the chemche gul (above) and the gorbaghe gul (bottom).

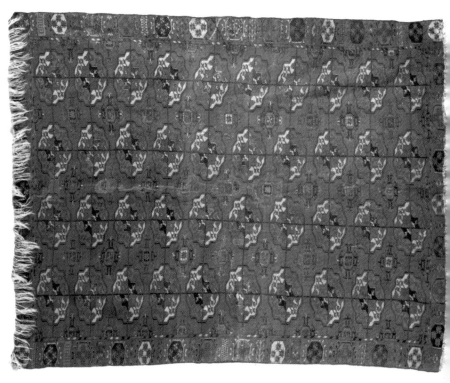

alternate with offset rows of other secondary, cruciform *guls*; these can be shaped like a "St. Andrew's cross," in which case they are strangely referred to as *chemche*, meaning "spoons," or they can be simple crosses, called *gorbaghe*, bearing an octagon with an eight-pointed star. The main borders usually have a series of octagons bearing four eight-pointed stars and are flanked by thin minor borders decorated with diagonal multicolour lines. Beginning around the middle of the 19th century, the importance of the borders, at least in terms of their number, and the

complexity of the designs on these carpets increased. Although the traditional designs and layouts remained unchanged, Tekke carpets underwent a general stylistic change during this period: the shapes went

from squares to rectangles, the fields narrowed, and the *guls* became smaller and were used more densely. This change was one of the signs of imminent crisis; the Tekke, the most powerful Turkoman tribe, were defeated between 1881 and 1885 by Russian troops. Today, Tekke carpets are among those most imitated in Pakistan and Afghanistan

Salor. Important examples made by this proud tribe are rare and can be recognized by their large round *gul*, known as a *Gulli gul*, meaning "flower *gul*," since it is characterized by the presence of an interior

Below: Detail of a Tekke carpet with typical full-field gul decoration; end 19th century. The traditional Tekke design began to grow denser around the second half of the 19th century.

Bottom: Salor sack decorated with typical tribal guls; second half 19th century. Tent sacks of this kind are called joval, *and carpets with this type of gul are also called Pendehs.*

trefoil motif, also found in the carpets of the Saryk and Ersari. This stylized floral element is repeated in each quarter of the *gul*, which is alternately coloured white/red and blue/pale red or blue/deep red. The scarlet red field is evenly spread with *Gulli guls* arranged in rows, but well spaced and without any connection among them; these alternate with much smaller minor *guls* shaped like flattened octagons. The main borders are decorated by the *kotchanak* motif or by characteristic double-T elements flanked by stepped medallions. Salor carpets are distinguished by a particular design found

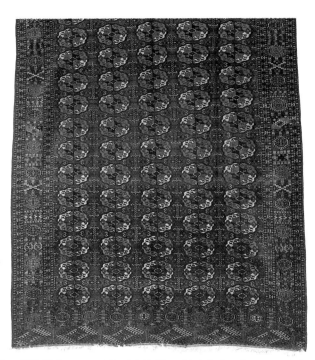

WESTERN TURKESTAN

Saryk carpet with full-field decoration of characteristic guls; 19th century. Saryks are distinguished by the presence of certain colours, such as orange and dark blue.

most of all in the tent sacks known as *joval*: this is the so-called Salor *gul*, characterized by a sharply defined octagon outlined with small triangular gablelike motifs. Rows of three Salor *guls* alternate with motifs composed of small black rectangles arranged to form a rhombus containing a star motif. Salor carpets bearing this design and datable to the second half of the 19th century are also called Pendehs, from the name of an oasis where the last Salor took refuge after fleeing the destruction of their tribe in 1856. The term *Pendeh* has ended up being used conventionally for the motif itself, which is also found in a more rigid and flattened form in carpets made by the Saryk and Tekke tribes.

Saryk. Saryk carpets, usually knotted with the symmetrical system, are distinguished chiefly by their colours, with dark blue and orange used in the designs; the fields of more recent examples are dark, passing from purple-red to brick-red. Saryk *guls* come in various forms more or less related to those of the Salor and Tekke, but the most characteristic *guls* are octagonal with twenty-four facets and decorated inside with cruciform elements or elements of some other style. Divided in quarters coloured white and orange

or light red, they are repeated full field in regular rows that alternate with secondary, usually cruciform *guls*. The borders are usually decorated with *kotchanak* and elaborate crosslike elements; the decoration of the minor

borders is more characteristic of this type and is composed of a typical motif of small multicolour triangles or horizontal-S motifs. A characteristic singular to this type is the frequent presence of two thin strips at the top of the

carpet decorated with tiny diagonal bars of various colours known as *gyak*.

Yomut. Usually made using the symmetrical knot, these carpets stand apart for the great variety of their designs, some of which belong to the classical Turkoman tradition and some of which show the influence of other traditions. Some of the *guls* are not only shaped differently from other *guls* but are also arranged differently, being distributed in alternate rows and coloured to create diagonal relationships. Some of the *guls* employed, such as the *tauk nuska gul*, octagonal in shape and characterized by the presence inside of four pairs of small extremely stylized animals, and the *dyrnak gul*, rhomboidal in form with typical hooked edges, belong to the Turkoman carpet language. Others show signs of external influence, such as a smaller type of *gul*, shaped like a toothed hexagon completed horizontally by two pairs of forked elements and decorated on the inside with small half moons, and the *kepse gul*, composed of five to seven large toothed segments in alternating colours arranged in steps that taken all together form a hexagon or rhombus. The main borders usually have white grounds with varied designs, such as frets,

The Turkoman ensi

Turkoman tribes use various kinds of knotted textiles for carrying out a wide range of tasks. Worthy of particular note are the carpets called ensi, which are used as door hangings for tents. They are characterized by a typical decoration based on a layout that is directional, rather than full-field like the remainder of Turkoman carpets, and has a single cross motif, usually ending in points, that divides the field into four panels enlivened by archaic designs that vary according to each tribe's traditions. Typical and frequent is a high border running on three sides and defined by a motif similar to a double T in white and black. The lower side is occupied by a high elam, which is another strip partly knotted and partly woven like a kilim, decorated by stylized floral motifs or by thin repeating geometric borders. The elam serves to protect the design of the field from wear caused by rubbing on the ground. The colours used in ensi are recognizable: the ground is dark red, the designs of the field are black, and those of the borders are white and sometimes include insertions in pale red. The traditional designs and colours have undergone transformations over time, beginning with reduction of the elam, but the ensi have never lost their distinguishing central cross motif. These carpets are related to the shamanistic beliefs of tribal culture, with the concept of the cosmic axis and a auspicious symbolism. The design of ensi is also called a hatchli (hadklu), which in Armenian means "cross."

*Below: Detail of
Yomut carpet with
full-field decoration of*
dyrnak guls; *19th
century.
Characteristics
include the minor
borders, decorated
with a hooked motif*

*similar to the
Caucasian running
dog.
Bottom: Detail of a
Chodor carpet with
full-field decoration of*
ertem guls; *end 19th
century.*

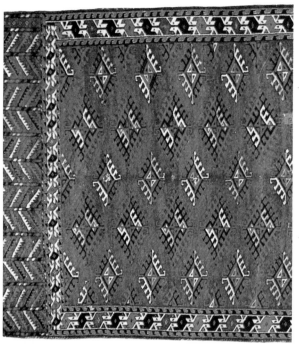

stylized curling leaves, and a typical "ship" motif composed of a geometric vine at the sides of which are elements of floral origin similar to small ships. The minor borders, aside from the usual horizontal-S motifs, are characterized by hooked motifs similar to the Caucasian running dog. Red and blue are the dominant colours in the designs, but also found are yellow, orange red, and, in the oldest specimens, a blue-green.

Chodor. The outstanding carpets from this production area are those decorated with the typical *ertem gul*, which is rhomboidal in shape with a stepped outline; inside it and decorating two of its outside ends are thin double-hooked motifs. This special small-size *gul* is repeated in staggered rows across the entire field, usually without secondary elements, but it is often enclosed within a thin grid of rhomboidal spaces. The *guls* are coloured to form alternating diagonal rows, usually in red and white on a light or dark red ground. The borders most common in Chodor carpets have a motif of vines with stylized curling leaves on a white ground; the minor borders usually have small multicolour horizontal-S motifs. Also occasionally encountered in Chodor carpets are numerous wide borders at one end.

Ersari. Carpets from this vast production area are distinguished by their lively and brilliant palette, mainly of yellow and intense red, but also including blue, blue-green, and black. These carpets also stand apart because of the variety of their motifs. Since they can be traced to both the Turkoman and Persian traditions they form two distinct groups. Those based on Turkoman traditions can be recognized by full-field decoration usually of three types: large octagonal *Gulli guls* with the classic trefoil designs; *termichin guls* with internal elements composed of small reciprocal triangles; or *tauk nuska guls.* Those based on Persian traditions are known conventionally as Beshir carpets, named either after the city of that name or the Ersari subtribe of that name. These are characterized by stylized floral decoration or by motifs borrowed from Persia and translated in geometric versions, such as *herati* and *mina khani* used full field and *boteh* arranged around a small round central medallion with four similar medallions located in the corners. Some carpets from this area are prayer rugs, a carpet type not native to Turkestan.

EASTERN TURKESTAN

♦ The stylistic elements that help to identify carpets from eastern Turkestan are the relatively small number of decorative motifs, the somewhat elementary geometric language (both abstract and stylized), and the decidedly lively colours, based primarily on red, blue, and yellow in all their tonalities. Although influenced by China, western Turkestan, Persia, and India, this production area succeeded over the centuries in keeping unchanged its own tradition, which is connected to pre-Islamic cultures, primarily Buddhist but also shamanistic. The layouts used most often are the superimposed-medallions with three medallions, full-field *guls*, saph (or "multiple-niche") carpets, and finally a local pomegranate-tree variety. The border decorations are extremely various, but the dominant motifs are the local trefoil, frets, and the T element. Typical of these carpets is a brick-red strip that runs around outside the borders. The spirit of these carpets is simple and elementary but at the same time robust and lively, secure in its solid tradition handed down over centuries. In examples made since the end of the 19th century, however, this joyfulness seems clouded by new colours in pastel tints.

The knotting system is asymmetrical, with a medium-low density of knots. Cotton is usually used for the foundation, while both wool and silk are used for the pile, and metallic threads are sometimes used together with the silk. The pile is usually trimmed medium-low. The shapes are very

Diagram of the asymmetrical knot, the system used in eastern Turkestan.

elongated: as a general rule, the length is nearly twice that of the width.

Major style types

Situated between western Turkestan and Mongolia, eastern Turkestan is today for the most part situated within the Chinese region of Sinkiang. Carpets from this region are conventionally called Samarkands, from the name of the Turkoman city located on the old silk route to China that was once a major center for the gathering of carpets that were then sold or exported, mostly to the West. Because of its location, Sinkiang was passed through by many peoples moving east or west and suffered many invasions by over the course of history, all of which influenced its

local art without, however, damaging its fidelity to the original geometric style and to the decorations descended from pre-Islamic culture.

The carpets of this area stem from an ancient tradition datable to as early as the 3rd century A.D. The earliest examples that have survived date to the end of the 18th century and were made in specialized workshops on both vertical and horizontal looms. These carpets present singular stylistic types. The most traditional, although not the most common, is the pomegranate-tree type, perhaps based on an ancient local design and believed to be symbolic of fertility, since those plants have abundant fruit and seeds. The field of these carpets is blue or light blue and covered by one or two intense red trees that grow from a small vase and extend upward geometric branches full of leaves and fruit. In many cases, the trees extend to the middle of field and are then repeated specularly, transforming the layout from directional to bidirectional. The most common compositional layout, however, is that of three medallions, for this arrangement is more closely connected to the local geometric taste and was probably influenced by Buddhist symbolism. These examples, usually with red grounds, are characterized by a row of three large

EASTERN TURKESTAN

Khotan carpet with three medallions; end 19th century. This layout, widespread in eastern Turkestan, is characterized by the particular round medallions (shown in the diagram below).

Also frequently used is the "wave" motif of the main border, symbol of the cosmos.

roundish octagonal medallions, usually coloured blue and bearing interior decoration of small stars, rosettes, stylized floral elements, or other geometric motifs. Much less frequent are layouts with central medallions or repeated medallions, but the medallions are always characterized by roundish octagonal forms. Somewhat widespread in eastern Turkestan is the saph, or "multiple-niche," layout, which probably represents an encounter between the local pre-Islamic iconographic tradition and the true Islamic tradition, since no single-niche prayer rugs have been found from this area. The niches appear in odd numbers and bear as interior decoration a stylized tree of life, pomegranates, floral decorations, or the geometric "herringbone" motif. There are also carpet types that show the

influence of motifs derived from other cultural contexts, such as *herati* (transformed into the typical "five-bud" motif) and floral elements from Persia, cloudbands and curvilinear grids from China, bunches of stylized flowers from India, and full-field *guls*

from western Turkestan. These *guls* are transformed, however, following local taste, from octagonal medallions into round rosettes with hooked edges. All the carpet types are completed by various kinds of borders that do not necessarily have any relationship to the primary motifs of the carpets. There are main borders with bicolour trefoil "wave" motifs, octagonal rosettes, stylized vines, or bunches of three geometric flowers arranged in rows with alternating bunches pointing in different directions. The minor borders are most often formed by geometric-abstract frets, swastikas, and T motifs.

Old carpets

Around 1870 two important phenomena brought about a major stylistic change in the carpets of eastern

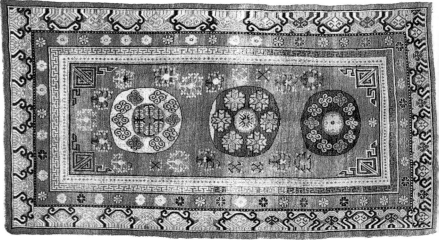

Khotan "five-bud" carpet; end 19th century. This type was influenced by the Persian herati motif and is typical of the oasis of Khotan. Typical of eastern Turkestan is the border with groups of flowers pointing in two directions.

The long, narrow carpets of Sinkiang

Aside from their designs and colours, the carpets of eastern Turkestan are characterized by their shape, which is long and narrow (usually almost twice as long as wide), with sizes more or less fixed at 40 x 80 inches. This shape was imposed by a precise practical necessity tied to daily life. Since earliest times, the main room in homes in Sinkiang has been a wide rectangular hall covered for almost its entire length by a wooden platform nearly a yard high on which the daily life of the house took place, on which family members slept, and where meetings were held. To make this platform as comfortable as possible, it was covered with one or two carpets, whose shapes had to be suitable to cover the shape of the platform. Carpets with squarer shapes have also been made in the production areas of eastern Turkestan. These carpets were made at the beginning of the 20th century to meet the powerful demand for carpets from the West. Thus their sizes were made to fit the different-shaped rooms of European and American homes, reaching on average 80-100 x 120-140 inches.

Turkestan: aniline dyes were introduced, and the carpets met with a favorable response when introduced to the great commercial market directed to the West. Results of these two factors included rigidity and confusion among the traditional designs and a transformation of the palette, which went from being lively and contrasting to being muted and harmonious. For this reason, carpets from the end of the 19th century are usually characterized by pastel tints, such as pale yellow, gray, violet, pale green, and pink. False "antique" carpets, made in the 19th century but known as "18th-century Samarkands," occasionally appear on the market. These are distinguished by pastel colours that have been artificially faded to simulate age and fool inexpert buyers. Of course, the colours of real

EASTERN TURKESTAN

Khotan carpet with a full-field curvilinear grid decoration; mid-19th century. The decorative motif was inspired by the Chinese ornamental heritage. Also common to Chinese taste are the large geometric borders composed of elaborate frets or T designs (shown in the diagram at bottom).

18th-century Sinkiang carpets are bright with sharp contrasts.

Major production areas

Carpets from eastern Turkestan, referred to collectively as Samarkands, are usually divided into three basic groups named for important oases: Kashgar, Yarkand, and Khotan. Given the general uniformity of designs from one area to another, close examination of structural characteristics is almost always necessary to determine a carpet's provenance.

Kashgar. Kashgar carpets are usually of refined quality and are generally datable to the period between the end of the 18th century and the middle of the 19th. Their styles reveal Persian and Chinese influences, and their colours are more delicate than those from the other two production areas.

Yarkand. These carpets can be identified by their weft strands, which are coloured blue or light blue. They often have pomegranate-tree designs, but there are also medallion layouts, carpets with *guls*, and saphs. The colours show sharp contrasts, as in the use of light yellow for the designs against red grounds.

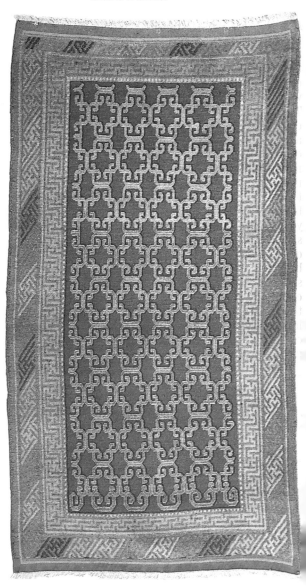

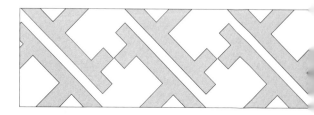

168

Below: Detail of Khotan medallion carpet; end 19th century. This is one of the most common layouts among the multiform production of the oasis of Khotan. Worthy of note is the well-defined interpretation of the "wave" motif in the border, as shown in the diagram.

Bottom: Yarkand two-medallion carpet; mid-19th century. A particular characteristic of Yarkands is the frequent use of pale yellow in the designs.

Khotan. These are the most recent of Samarkands (datable to the end of the 19th century) and also the most various and numerous. There are examples of every design type, although the most common layouts use three medallions or a cental medallion. The palette tends toward brick red or blue for grounds, and yellow, sky blue, or various shades of red for the designs. Khotans can also be identified by their weft strands, which are coloured brown, and by their knotting, which is less dense than that on carpets from the other production areas.

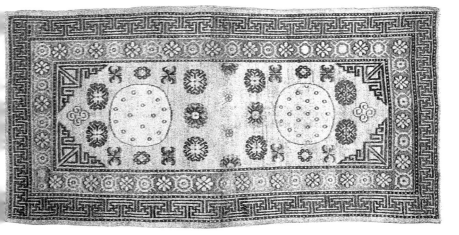

EASTERN TURKESTAN

■ TEKKE ■

Carpet with geometric decoration; 18th century. Typical: border and Tekke *guls* repeated in the field.

SARYK

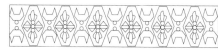

Carpet with geometric decoration; 19th century. Typical: the border and the Saryk *guls* repeated in the field.

SALOR

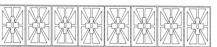

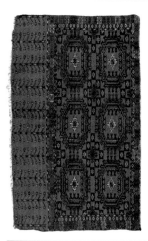

Carpet with geometric decoration; 19th century. Typical: the border and the Salor *guls* repeated in the field.

YOMUT

Carpet with geometric decoration; 19th century. Typical: the border and the Yomut *guls* repeated in the field.

WESTERN TURKESTAN

19th-century carpets

YARKAND

Pomegranate-tree carpet; mid-19th century. Typical: border with rosettes and repeated pomegranate motif.

KHOTAN

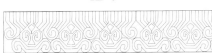

Carpet with three medallions; end 19th century. Typical: the border with waves and the round medallions.

KHOTAN

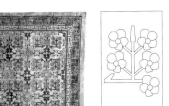

"Five-bud" carpet; end 19th century. Typical: the border and the motif with five flowers repeated in the field.

KHOTAN

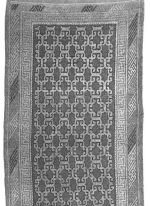

Grid carpet; mid-19th century. Typical: the border and the curvilinear grid of the field.

INDIA

♦ The primary aspect that characterizes Indian carpets is their singular, intense palette, based on yellow, pink, light blue, and green and best displayed in the typical bluish red known as lac red, used only for the grounds of fields. The designs, although indebted to the Persian style, are distinguished by their asymmetry and strong sense of the pictorial, with close attention to reality and detail. The decoration shows a preference for naturalistic floral designs and figural scenes arranged on directional layouts, and the compositions are not elaborate; the most common layouts involve full-field distributions using rows or grids, in-and-out palmettes, and prayer rugs. Because of this naturalistic taste, Indian carpets lack characteristic decorative motifs, aside from those few borrowed from Persia or other production areas, such as *herati*, *boteh*, and cloudbands. The general character that informs these carpets is thus very rich, aristocratic, and refined, though without the ideal or abstract elegance common to the Persian manner, and seeming instead concrete and exuberant, with a sensibility that verges on the carnal.

All Indian carpets are made using the asymmetrical knot and stand apart technically

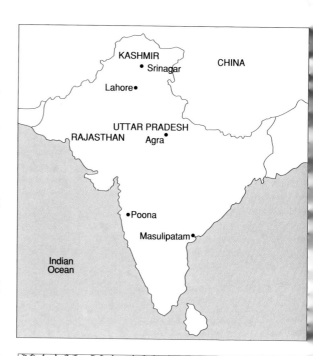

Diagram of the asymmetrical knot used in India.

because of their particularly dense knotting, well suited to rendering realistic figural details. The foundation is usually of cotton and the pile wool; in northern regions the soft and shiny wool of Kashmir is used. Sometimes silk is used both in the foundation and for the pile. The pile is usually trimmed low. The carpets are usually medium or large in size, reaching as much as 150 x 240 inches.

172

Opposite: Map of
India showing the
major production
centers.
Borders typical of
India: floral with
masks (above) and
naturalistic floral
(below).

Below: Animal carpet;
early 17th century.
Typical of the Indian
style is the
naturalistic intent:
depicted on the field
are storks, peacocks,
phoenixes, turtle
doves, and hoopoes.

Also characteristic of
Indian carpets is the
particular intense red
ground with bluish
reflections, obtained
using a particular
variety of cochineal
called lac, which gives
lac red.

object of furnishing designed
to beautify the palaces of the
Mogul court. Because of this
close connection to the
Mogul court, the knotted
carpet was inevitably
destined to decline when
that court declined, which it
began to do toward the end
of the 18th century.

The Indian carpet came
into being to serve the same
purposes as the "classic"
Persian carpet and, in fact,
imitated both Persian
technique and style:
asymmetrical knots with fine
knotting; use of precious
materials, such as the
highest-quality wool from
Kashmir and sometimes
even silk and gold and silver
threads; production based on
cartoons furnished by court
miniaturists; curvilinear
style; and designs of the
floral and figural character.

Given the lack of intact
examples from the 16th
century, the most important
existing records of this
direct dependence on the
art of Persia is offered by
the so-called Indo-Isfahan
or Indo-Persian carpets,
datable to the 17th and 18th
centuries and characterized
by Safavid designs
composed of in-and-out
palmettes, *herati*, and
sometimes cloudbands in
orderly full-field
arrangements. Initially
attributed to Persia, and
more precisely to Herat,
these carpets were later
divided into two groups
based on their palettes and

Birth of the Indian carpet

Probably because of the
region's warm climate,
which does not require
protection from cold, the
knotted carpet was
unknown in India until the
16th century. Indeed, the
knotted carpet exists in
India not because of an age-
old tradition but because of
an act of importation,
carried out by the emperor
Akbar (reigned 1556-1605).

Akbar, the greatest ruler of
the Mogul dynasty (1526/27-
1858), was an admirer of
Safavid art and had artists
and artisans sent from the
Persian court to set up
specialized workshops in
Agra and Fatehpur Sikri, the
two capitals of his empire, as
well as in Lahore, in modern-
day Pakistan. Therefore in
India the knotted carpet
originated as a product made
exclusively for the court and
conceived of as a precious

levels of calligraphic sense: those with the most intense colours, with lac-red grounds and designs with pale outlines or no outlines at all, were taken to show Indian sensibility, and the others were said to show Persian taste. Since these are such minor differences, the recent tendency has been to leave provenance undecided and to see these carpets as proof of the close relationship between the Safavid and Mogul courts and attribute them to a common Indo-Persian style.

The Mogul style

Over the course of the 17th century, as local miniaturists and artists slowly replaced the Persian artists and artisans in the great workshops, a more specifically Indian character began to develop in the Indian carpet, rendering it less dependent on Persia and better suited to representing the taste and needs of the region.

The Mogul style was influenced by the passion for botany of Akbar's son,

the emperor Jahangir (reigned 1605-1627). Under his rule all the arts tended toward representations of a floral character, which were rendered with such naturalism and presented such a variety of species that they competed with Western herbals. Under the reign of Jahangir's son and successor, Shah Jahan (reigned 1628-1658), this style reached full expressive maturity, evident in the perfect realism of its renderings and close attention to detail.

174

Figural carpet; early 17th century. This type, common to Persia, was distinguished in India by the asymmetrical arrangement, the dominance of the figures over the ground, and the choice of scenes of activity.

Mogul carpets are thus distinguished principally by their highly realistic and detailed floral and animal subjects, made possible by the use of very dense and minute knotting on foundations of cotton and sometimes silk. The flowers and flowering plants represented are neither imaginary nor in any sense abstract, as are those on Persian carpets, but instead belong to the real world of nature; in the same way, the dragons and other legendary beasts that appear are hardly successful, while the real animals, particularly those native to India, such as elephants, tigers, cheetahs, and rhinoceroses, dominate the designs.

All these decorative elements are usually arranged in directional layouts in which they are distributed in an absolutely asymmetrical fashion, which ignores the compositional rigor of Persian carpets. The area of the carpet is not densely occupied by designs and much less by arabesques, but is well balanced between full and empty spaces, without any *horror vacui*, but rather with the precise intention of making the ground and its particular colour stand out.

Carpets in the Mogul style can also be recognized by their distinctive palette, a result of the great skills of Indian dyers, who were capable of obtaining, usually by means of repeated dyeings, singular shades and colours so intense they seem enameled. Typical of Indian carpets is lac red, with its characteristic bluish reflections, obtained from an insect of the cochineal family known as lac and used in grounds; against this colour stand out designs coloured light yellow, mustard yellow, light red, pink, light blue, midnight blue, light green, emerald green, orange, black, and brown.

Another particularity of these carpets is the way colours are combined, for this is done without outlines, even when two different tones of the same tint are used side by side, such as red and pink or blue and light blue. The borders are characterized by a dark

INDIA

Drawing taken from a figural carpet of the 17th century. Elephants are a way of identifying Indian carpets, for they are the animal most representative of that land.

ground, rendered using a strong green-blue, suitable for making contrasts with the lac red of the field.

Antique types

Almost all existing antique Indian carpets are held in major collections or museums; datable to the 16th to 17th centuries, they can be grouped into decorative types that show varying degrees of debt to central or eastern Persia. Given their stylistic uniformity, the areas where they were made cannot be established with certainty.

Floral carpets

Floral carpets are the most common type, and most are attributed to Lahore. The flowering plants, often of many different species, are arranged full field within a grid, the shape of which varies, or are arranged in the more typically Mogul style of horizontal rows. In one 18th-century layout, the flowers are made small and presented in dense arrangements, each flower joined to another by extensions of its stem, a scheme directly reminiscent of Persian floral carpets. Also included in this type are the Indo-Isfahan carpets and certain rare examples with trees, which are often presented with flowering foliage.

Figural carpets

The subjects of figural carpets sometimes reproduce episodes from Indian epics but more often present hunting scenes. These carpets have greater vitality than Persian figural carpets in part because of the asymmetrical distribution of their elements but primarily because of the size and pictorial importance given the figures with respect to the floral ground. Furthermore, the figures are usually shown in movement. Typically Indian is the presence of an elephant, and characteristic of these carpets is the design of the border, often curiously enlivened by grotesque masks. Included within this group are examples decorated with the waq-waq tree.

Prayer rugs

The Mogul interpretation of the prayer rug, a type

foreign to Indian religious life, shows the traits characteristic of Mogul style. Although clearly influenced by Persia, Mogul prayer rugs are composed of a highly articulated mihrab, the interior field of which is coloured lac red and bears Mogul flowering plants, shown in large size to indicate the realistic transformation of the symbolic tree of life. In the so-called *millefleurs* prayer rugs, datable to the 18th century, the field is instead thickly covered by myriad tiny flowers of diverse species and always growing from a single plant; the niche of these rugs is often flanked by two typical cypresses.

Portuguese carpets

The so-called Portuguese carpets, discussed among the types of Persian carpets, are variously attributed to northern or southern Persia or to the Portuguese colony in Goa, India. Aside from the people in European dress that appear on these carpets, the Indian provenance hypothesis is supported by the particularly intense and brilliant colours. In the absence of certain proof, however, the production area for these carpets remains obscure.

176

The 19th century

Having entered a crisis at the end of the 18th century, Indian carpet making suffered during the 19th century from the usual changes involved in meeting market demands, which in India meant the tired repetition of Mogul models or their betrayal in favor of European subjects or, more often, the imitation of classic Persian motifs that had already become established on the Western market. In addition, during this same period the local carpet workshops were taken over and directed by English or European companies. Even so, Indian carpets maintained their high technical levels until 1860-1870, when the introduction of chemical dyes made even the renowned Indian colours begin to lose their intensity.

Since the region does not have an ancient tradition of carpet making, and since carpets were not made at any level there until the 16th century, India can boast of no nomad or village carpets. All the "old" examples that have survived until today were made in city workshops, but given their general stylistic homogeneity, production areas cannot be established with any accuracy. Referred to commercially and conventionally as Agra carpets, from the name of the city, Indian carpets can be broadly divided into geographical regions on the basis of the quality of their wool: if it is soft and shiny, the carpet probably comes from a northern region; if the wool is rough and opaque, it probably comes from a southern region. The leading workshops of the many that were active during the 19th century include the northern ones of Lahore, Srinagar, and the regions of Rajasthan and Uttar Pradesh, with Agra; the central ones of Poona; and finally the southern ones in the area of Masulipatam.

CHINA

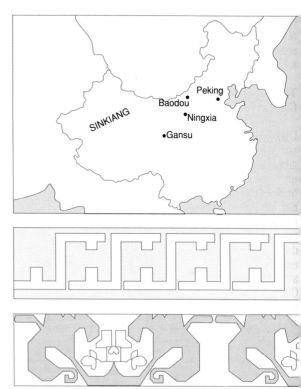

♦ Many aspects of Chinese carpets make them stand out against the vast stylistic panorama of Oriental carpets. In fact, Chinese carpets are immediately identifiable because of these singular aspects, beginning with their decorative motifs, which appear suspended on the field, unattached to one another and without strong outlines. The palette is restricted and neither lively nor contrasting; it is limited to six basic tints and all their various shadings, and these colours are used in accordance with a singular sensitivity directed at creating harmonious and delicate arrangements dominated by yellow and blue. Finally, the style employed does not show the usual and insurmountable discrimination between the geometric language and the floral but lives in a happy medley of the two. The designs are of both the geometric-abstract and the naturalistic type, but they are distinguished by their symbolic character. The

The asymmetrical knot, the only system used in China.

most common layouts are the central medallion, the "four-and-one" medallion, various kinds of grids, and those with motifs arranged more or less symmetrically. The borders, conceived as frames for the carpet, bear a wide variety of motifs, prominent among them peonies and other floral decorations, various symbols, frets, swastikas, and T designs.

The technical characteristics of Chinese carpets also set them apart from other Oriental carpets. They are knotted with the asymmetrical knot with a particularly low density of coarse knots. To hide the roughness of the cotton foundation, the wool pile is trimmed somewhat high. At the beginning of the 20th century the practice began of cutting the pile to make the designs stand out further. Special shears designed for the purpose are used to cut around the outlines of the figures, and this cutting sometimes goes farther and involves trimming the pile to different heights, leaving the areas of the decorations higher than the ground areas. Antique carpets tend to be squarish (75 x 100 inches on average), while more recent examples are of varying forms and are sometimes quite large (115 x 150 inches on average).

The carpet and official Chinese art

Carpet making was not accepted as one of the great courtly arts in China until around the second half of the 17th century, much later than in any of the other areas of Oriental carpet making. The late date can be partially explained by the limited availability of wool in China, but it is primarily a result of the specific characteristics of knotting, which do not permit the full translation of China's aesthetic canons, which

tend to favour the rendering of fine detail and calligraphic perfection. This was not a matter of introducing a new product from abroad, as had happened in India, but of raising to a higher level a product known and used for centuries, by at least part of the Chinese population. In fact, the technique of knotting was probably introduced in China during ancient times by the central Asian peoples who invaded the northwestern provinces. The tradition of Chinese carpet making was developed in those northwestern provinces, and even when the official culture began to take an interest in carpets, the

production of carpets continued to be circumscribed within the northeastern regions, where it was practiced in private workshops. Although not developed in specialized court workshops, the art of the Chinese carpet progressed, always following the general aesthetic canons of Chinese art and the wishes of the ruling class.

The style of Chinese carpets

The style of Chinese carpets is very different from that of carpets made in Islamic countries, and this difference begins with the general concept of the composition. In China, the

space of the carpet is not conceived as an empty area that must be completely filled with decorations joined one to another, but is understood instead as a simple support for traditional designs that exist independently from one another, with no ornamental ties and no *horror vacui.* In Chinese thinking every art form represents only another vehicle for expressing universal concepts using codified symbolic motifs, and these motifs always maintain their individual meaning, regardless of their context or relationship to other symbols. In this way the field is conceived as a flexible space in which the various traditional designs are suspended individually.

Even so, the designs are always regulated by a compositional layout, even when there are so few of them that there almost seems to be no layout.

The Chinese decorative language, which seeks calligraphic perfection, is expressed in carpets using both the geometric and floral styles. The two styles are combined with such refined skill that they create not a hybrid or confused language but one that is balanced and elegant, composed of rigidly geometric motifs and others that are softly curvilinear. The layouts used most often are the central medallion accompanied by four corner medallions and the "four-and-one" medallion. The medallion is conceived in a singular way, however, and has no definite form and is not completed by pendants; rather, it is composed of the assembly of several elements, such as mythical animals, flowers, or geometric figures, all grouped together usually in a circle, and often without any enclosing line to contain them with precision. The grid layout, a typically Chinese form, is used a great deal in antique examples. It involves a geometric grid spread across the entire field; the grid is composed of various shapes, such as swastikas, "round parentheses," or the special "grain of rice"

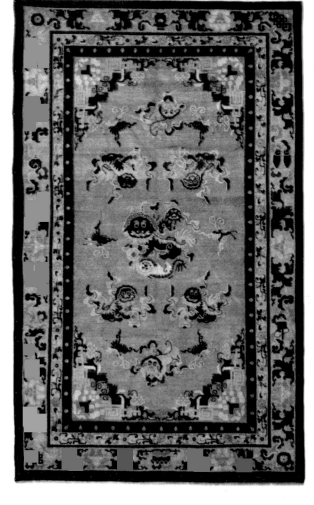

Below: Detail of a carpet
with geometric
decoration; 18th century.
The field is enlivened by
a curvilinear grid,
formed by the repetition
of a motif similar to
rounded parentheses.

Bottom: Medallion
carpet; end 19th-early
20th century. The
cruciform medallion
is surrounded by
naturalistic elements,
including flowers,
butterflies, and birds,
arranged

symmetrically. Note
the main border,
decorated with
flowering vines
(peonies) and vases.

motifs, which are composed of small oblique segments, arranged to point in all four directions. There are also full-field decorations using naturalistic floral motifs, in particular the often used classic peony and lotus flower. Another popular layout is distinguished by the presence on the field of various symbolic figures.

Column carpets, so-called because they were made to be tied around the columns in Buddhist temples in place of paintings, constitute an absolutely original genre. They were made so that when fixed in place around a column their decoration would progress in a continuous way, with dragons twisting around the column accompanied by other important religious and philosophical symbolic elements, all of them widely spaced.

Unlike the Islamic border, the Chinese border is not understood as a fundamental element to complete the field but simply as an unimportant frame to be filled with floral or geometric motifs, often in harmonic contrast with the design in the field. Among the designs most often used in main borders are various frets, often presented with three-dimensional effects; swastikas; T motifs; and floral motifs, such as peonies or lotus flowers,

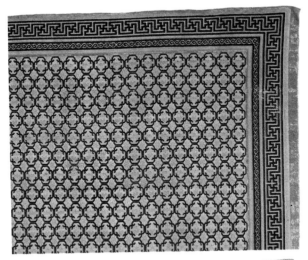

Medallion carpet; end 19th-early 20th century. The medallion and corners are formed of groupings of various Chinese symbols, among which are the endless knot, the lotus, fish, and castanets. At the bottom of the main border are Taoist symbols, the sword, the fan, the flute, and the bamboo basket.

Old carpets

After its period of greatest splendour, attested to by the surviving examples datable to between the 18th and early 19th century, the Chinese carpet began a slow process of decline. The carpets made after 1860-1870 show the signs of enslavement to Western taste: the motifs arc less pure, less refined, and more affected; and the colours are in a wide range of pastel tones, thanks to the introduction of chemical dyes. The field is either too empty or is overfilled; the borders are enlarged and complicated; the grounds are almost all blue, and the knotting, while more refined, is less traditional.

During the second half of the 19th century the imperial factories, such as that of Peking, and the many other factories directed by Western entrepreneurs began to replace the small provincial workshops. The efforts to meet increasing commercial demands gradually led to the decadence and finally the death of the traditional Chinese carpet. The final expiration of the true Chinese carpet occurred around 1920. At that time landscapes and human figures were first introduced to the decoration of carpets, but even more important was the preference shown a hybrid genre, an imitation

rendered in a naturalistic manner. One of the characteristic decorations of the minor borders is known as the "pearl" motif and is composed of small white disks that usually appear on a blue ground. Also noteworthy is the use of an outer guard, which is brown in the oldest examples and blue in later ones, datable to the beginning of the 19th century onward.

The palette of Chinese carpets is markedly different from that of Islamic carpets, for it is not based on variety, vivacity, or contrast, and knows nothing of the marked predominance of red found in Islamic works. Chinese taste is based on several basic tints, including yellow, blue, white, light red, black, and brown, making capable use of the possible shadings, so as to obtain harmonious and elegant effects, such as light yellow on gilded yellow or apricot pink on salmon red. The predominant colours are yellow and blue, symbols, respectively, of the earth and the sky. In carpets from before the second half of the 19th century, the ground of the field is almost exclusively yellow, while it is usually a deep blue in later carpets.

Chinese symbols

The ancient motifs found on Chinese carpets are decorative in only a small way, since by nature they are fundamentally symbolic. In China, the artistic language is composed primarily of symbols common to all the artistic genres and techniques. Their meaning has remained unchanged over the centuries, but interpreting them successfully is not at all easy, in part because they are a great many of them. Some have been drawn from the natural world, others from ancient local myths, and yet others from the Buddhist and Taoist religions; a small number are composed of more or less complicated abstract designs. The most common symbols are the dragon (union of the earthly and celestial forces and the emperor), the phoenix (immortality and the empress), the Fo-dog (protection from evil), lotus flower (purity and summer), the peony (respect and wealth), the stag and stork (longevity), the cloud (divine power), the mountain and water (stability on a stormy sea), the bat (fortune, since its name phonetically resembles anfu, "fortune"), the swastika (cosmic rotation), and the ideograms Shou and Fu (fortune). Typical of column carpets are the eight Buddhist symbols: the canopy (royalty), the lotus (prosperity), the umbrella (authority, good government), the shell (victory), the wheel (the route to salvation), the vase (harmony) two fish (happiness and utility), and the endless knot (longevity and destiny). There are also eight Taoist symbols: the sword (victory), the staff and gourd (healing), the fan (immortality), the basket of flowers (magic), castanets (soothing music), the flute (miracles), the lotus (prosperity), and bamboo and staffs (foresight and fortune).

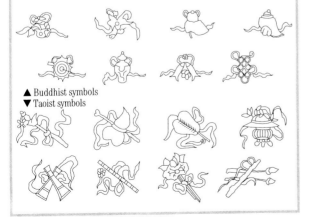

▲ Buddhist symbols
▼ Taoist symbols

of the 17th-century floral French carpets produced in the factories of Savonnerie and Aubusson. Several technical stratagems were involved in the creation of this hybrid genre, such as the differentiated trimming of the pile (higher for the decorative motifs) and cutting around the outlines of the designs, both systems introduced to make the decorations stand out against the ground.

Major production areas

Because of the general stylistic homogeneity of Chinese carpets, determining the provenance of a carpet based on design alone is not at all easy; however, chromatic and technical differences, along with some stylistic variations, have permitted the identification of several similar groups that can be attributed—albeit amid a thousand uncertainties—to specific production areas. Most of these few production areas are located in the northwest, the area traditionally associated with the production of carpets.

Area of Ningxia. The carpets produced in this area are considered the classic Chinese carpets, the most antique and thus the best; they are distinguished by motifs rendered in a pure style, by yellow or at the most pink grounds, and by

Medallion carpet; modern workmanship. This example is in the hybrid style developed during the 1920s in imitation of 17th-century French carpets with floral motifs; it was made using the new techniques of trimming the pile to differing heights and cutting out the designs.

prevalently blue designs. The term *Ningxia* has been much abused, to the point that all Chinese carpets are divided into those from Ningxia and those made later, datable to the early 20th century; the term is used commercially as a definition of quality. Technically, these carpets are distinguished by the density of their knots, which is very low with respect to all other Chinese carpets, and for their somewhat soft foundations. The decorative motifs used include all the characteristic types common to Chinese carpets.

Area of Gansu. Carpets from this area have lively colours and decorations that resemble those of eastern Turkestan, as is indicated in the widespread use of the superimposed-medallions layout using three medallions shaped like roundish octagons. Typical of the area is the *bulo* motif, which is composed of tiny red, white, and blue disks spread across the field. In general, the fields are blue with the designs in bright red or orange.

Area of Baodou. Made only at the end of the 19th century, these carpets are distinguished by their dense workmanship, small sizes, and decoration. This decoration was initially based primarily on stylized designs and then later was based on realistic motifs, such as landscapes and human figures. The grounds are usually red.

Peking. This carpet factory was set up around 1860 and made a vast number of carpets. These carpets, somewhat large and thick, usually have blue, beige, or ivory grounds decorated with bunches of naturalistic flowers, various symbols, and central medallions, often composed of landscape elements.

Below left: Detail of Gansu medallion carpet; early 20th century. The style imitates that of eastern Turkestan, evident most of all in the shape of the roundish octagonal medallion.

The bulo *motif, composed of small disks spread across the field, is typical of the Gansu area.*
Below right: Three-medallion carpet; end 19th century.
Bottom: Carpet with

floral decoration; end 19th century. The untraditional colours and, even more, the superabundant decoration of the field date this example to the end of the 19th century.

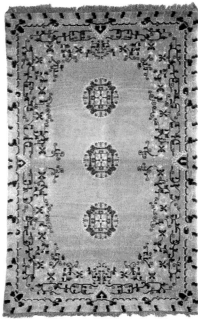

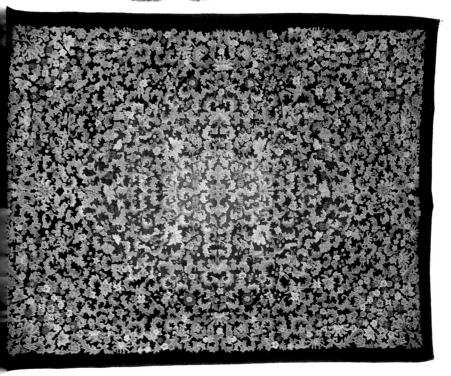

THE WEST

♦ The only European nation that can boast an ancient tradition of carpet making, noted since the 12th century, is Spain, as a result of its long Arab domination. Spanish carpets are distinguished by the so-called Spanish knot and by the preference for red, yellow, and blue. These carpets initially took inspiration from Anatolian geometric motifs, but the coats of arms of local noble families were added to these in the 15th century, as seen in the carpets of Alcaraz. During the 16th century preference was given to floral motifs based on those of contemporary fabrics, and perfect copies of Oriental examples were made in Cuenca during the 17th century. During the 18th century the production, by then in crisis, was taken over by the great royal factories of Madrid, which imposed the symmetrical knot and imitation of the formal French style.

In France, a great state carpet-making factory was set up in 1672 in an old soap works, the Savonnerie, near Paris. In 1712 it was transformed into the Royal Factory of Furniture and Carpets in the Style of Persia and the Levant, and in 1825 it was joined to the national factory of Gobelins. Made with the symmetrical knot, Savonnerie carpets are technically

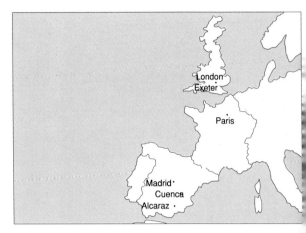

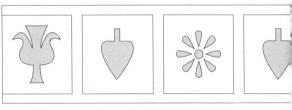

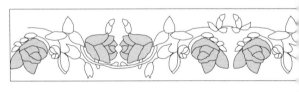

Diagram of the Spanish, or single-warp, knot used in Spain.

distinguished by foundations in hemp or linen, by knots cut in rows by being wrapped in series around a cutting bar, and by great sizes, suitable to the enormous halls of the court. Their designs are unrelated to Oriental motifs and follow instead the evolution of French taste, echoing the friezes and stuccowork of architectural ornament and closely following the styles of the furniture they were made to be draped over, from baroque and rococo to Art Nouveau and Art Deco.

Opposite: Map of Europe. Spain, France, and England are the historical homelands of carpet making in Europe. Borders typical of European carpets: Spanish border with

stylized designs enclosed in geometric compartments (above); characteristic French border with naturalistic floral vine (below).

Below: Carpet with geometric decoration; Alcaraz, 15th century. The Spanish style is distinguished by its geometric character and the predominance of red, yellow, and blue.

Heraldic coats of arms often appear as well.

The name Savonnerie indicates knotted carpets of extreme luxury; the name Aubusson indicates flatweaving, that of the tapestry, which is less costly and is made by small workshops to satisfy a "middle-class" market. Less precious and made in various shapes, Aubussons were produced from the middle of the 18th century onward and followed the stylistic evolution of Savonnerie carpets, standing apart from these by simpler and less refined designs. The style of both the Savonnerie and Aubusson carpets— their curvilinear designs, naturalistic floral friezes (garlands, vines, scattered flowers), and generally pale and shaded colours—had so much influence on overseas production that between the end of the 18th century and the early 19th century the French carpet became the model to imitate, even in the Orient (especially in Anatolia and China). Like all other European carpet makers, however, those of France went into crisis around the second half of the 19th century.

Around the middle of the 18th century carpet factories of a certain importance were set up in England, among them those of Fulham and Exeter. At the end of the century the workshops of Thomas Moore and Thomas Whitty met with particular success. The architect

Below: Detail of a *Savonnerie carpet with floral decoration; 19th century. Made using the technique of knotting, Savonnerie carpets are outstanding among French carpets, and* their flowers and roses had a profound impact on Oriental carpets during the 19th century, as did their colours, which are generally light or pastel.

Bottom: Savonnerie carpet with naturalistic decoration; early 19th century. The roses and swans of this carpet represent some of the motifs introduced by Napoleon's wife Josephine Beauharnais.

Robert Adam worked for both of these, and in his designs conferred special importance on floors, conceiving them as mirrors for ceilings. The carpets he designed therefore follow the rules of architectural decoration of the period, the neoclassical, and bear sober motifs taken from the ancients. At the beginning of the 19th century an exotic style, influenced by Chinese motifs, was created in Axminister. These efforts were not to last, however, for around 1850 the general decline of the hand-made knotted carpet began in Europe, caused both by competition from Western-style Oriental carpets and the new techniques of mechanical looms. Although sporadic attempts were made, manual knotting was soon abandoned throughout Europe in favor of the more economic industrial production with designs inspired by those of Oriental carpets.

Bibliography

Allane, Lee. *Oriental Rugs: A Buyer's Guide*. London: Thames and Hudson, 1988.
Black, David, ed. *The Macmillan Atlas of Rugs & Carpets*. New York: Macmillan, 1985.
Dimand, M. S. *Oriental Rugs in the Metropolitan Museum of Art*. New York: Metropolitan
Museum of Art, 1973.
Hawley, Walter A. *Oriental Rugs, Antique and Modern*. Reprint of 1913 edition. New York:
Dover Publications, 1970.
Rostov, Charles I., and Guanyan, Jia. *Chinese Carpets*. New York: Harry N. Abrams, 1983.

Photo credits

The abbreviations a (above), b (bottom), c (center), l (left), and r (right) refer to the
position of the illustration on the page.

Museums and collections

Cleveland Museum of Art: 51, 79, 83, 89bl,
91bl, 91br, 116, 147a
Giacomo Cohen and sons collection, Rome:
10, 45b, 52, 53a, 74, 76a, 87b, 117a, 119,
120bl, 125, 127bl, 130al, 144l, 155, 159a, 160,
161, 169a, 181b, 182, 184, 185b
Hermitage, St. Petersburg: 12
Historiska Museum, Stockholm: 30b
Islamisches Museum, Berlin: 66, 88al
G. Mandel collection, Milan: 34ar, 42, 75,
88br, 122al, 162a, 163
Hamburgisches Museum für Volkerkunde,
Hamburg: 29al, 157, 158, 159b
Metropolitan Museum of Art, New York: 8
(Rogers Fund), 29ar, 61, 96b, 100, 174ar,
177bl, 181a
Musée des Arts Décoratifs, Paris: 69b, 102
Museo Bardini, Florence (photos Arborio
Mella), 31, 38, 43, 60a, 65, 67b, 69a, 72, 88al,
88ar, 91ar, 105, 106, 139
Museo Civico of San Gimignano, Siena: 70
Museum of the Carpet, Teheran (G.
Mandel): 81, 110
Museo Nazionale del Bargello, Florence: 63,
64, 89ar

Museo Poldi Pezzoli, Milan (photos Arborio
Mella): 27b, 35, 94a, 99, 101
Museo S. Marco, Venice: 107
Museum für Islamische Kunst, Berlin: 28b,
37a, 37b, 59, 67a, 68b, 73, 77
Museum für Kunst und Kulturgeschichte,
Lubeck: 25a
Museum of Fine Arts, Boston: 175
National Gallery, London: 60b
Oesterreichisches Museum für angewandte
Kunst, Vienna: 9, 28a, 62, 98, 108, 173, 174al
Philadelphia Museum of Art: 103, 187
Royal Ontario Museum (Bequest of Mrs. F.
W. Cowan): 179
Textile Museum, Washington: 138
Türk ve Islam Müzesi, Istanbul: 58
Victoria and Albert Museum, London: 27a,
96a, 97

Photographers

The publisher wishes to thank the Archivio
Fotografico Mondadori and Maurizio Cohen
for supplying photographs. Special thanks
go to the Finarte and Sotheby's auction
houses for their generous cooperation.

INDEX

Numbers in *italics* refer to illustrations.